# HOW
# UDAY KOTAK
# BUILT A VALUABLE
# INDIAN BANK

# HOW
# UDAY KOTAK
# BUILT A VALUABLE
# INDIAN BANK

R.Gopalakrishnan
Tulsi Jayakumar

RUPA

Published by
Rupa Publications India Pvt. Ltd 2021
7/16, Ansari Road, Daryaganj
New Delhi 110002

*Sales centres:*
Allahabad Bengaluru Chennai
Hyderabad Jaipur Kathmandu
Kolkata Mumbai

ISBN: 978-93-90547-75-3

First impression 2021

10 9 8 7 6 5 4 3 2 1

The moral right of the authors has been asserted.

# Contents

# Preface

This book, *How Uday Kotak Built a Valuable Indian Bank* is the last volume in the series titled *Shapers of Business Institutions* that probes the mindset, behaviour and actions of Shapers of Institutions. The series looks at iconic Gen-L institutions that started or flourished around the time of India's liberalization. The fact that this is the last book of the series is also apt, as Kotak Mahindra Bank is the youngest among all the institutions we studied for the book series. And yet, in less than two decades since its establishment, it has risen to become one of the most-valued banks in India in terms of market capitalization.[1] It is also the most expensive bank stock in the world.[2]

Researching and writing about how Uday Kotak set up this enterprise with his leadership team has been exciting and educative, especially at a time when the Indian banking sector has been under much scrutiny and stress. Success

---

[1] 'Top 10 most-valued banks in India in terms of market capitalisation.' *CNBCTV18*, 9 May 2019, https://www.cnbctv18.com/photos/market/stocks/top-10-most-valued-banks-in-india-in-terms-of-market-capitalisation-3239461.htm. Accessed 4 July 2020.

[2] 'Kotak Mahindra is now the most expensive bank stock in world, Financial Express.' *Financial Express*, 22 May 2020, https://www.financialexpress.com/market/kotak-mahindra-emerges-as-most-expensive-bank-stock-in-world/1966850/. Accessed 4 July 2020.

in banking, especially in times of an economic slowdown, depends heavily on trust. Trust is the oxygen on which banks live, thrive and build their brand franchise.

## WHAT IS THERE IN A NAME?

Even historically, two centuries ago, banks were essentially merchant banks, engaged principally in handling and discounting of trade bills.[3] Firms such as JP Morgan and Goldman Sachs in the United States of America or Rothschild and SG Warburg in Britain started off as partnership firms, bearing the names of the partners—much like firms in accountancy and law. Retail banks, formed later, often carried generic or place names such as Citibank, National Westminster and Royal Bank of Scotland.

Among Indian banks, the golden oldies that have been around for about a century are mostly in the public sector. Brand names of Indian retail banks too, are usually generic rather than named after a founder. For example, Central Bank of India was founded by Sir Sorabjee Pochkhanawala and Sir Pherozeshah Mehta, but this fact is buried in a historian's crypt rather than expressed in the brand name of the bank. Even the newer Indian banks in the private sector bear an institutional promoter's name or a neutral name; for example, ICICI Bank, HDFC Bank, Axis Bank, Yes Bank or Bandhan Bank. In this space therefore, Kotak Mahindra Bank is unique because its brand bears the founder's name along with a prominent

---

[3]Bill Discounting is a method of trading the bill of exchange with the financial institution before its maturity, at a price lower than its value. The discount on the bill of exchange depends on the time remaining for its maturity and also the risk involved in its repayment.

industrialist's name. Two centuries ago, if a well-known family attached its name to a bank, it must have been reassuring to potential customers. Just as it has proved to be today.

Parentage matters. Modern banks are designed and built to be institutions, resting solidly on the twin pillars of transparency and dependability. Therefore, the legacy of established brand names like ICICI or HDFC is a great asset to a bank. For a brand-new bank, the names of Kotak and Mahindra provide a startling degree of reassurance. Our book describes how Uday Kotak had wanted to demonstrate commitment to his venture by placing his own name in the title. He also persuaded an established industrial house to join his banking venture. Trust had to be built, brick by brick, *ab initio*, and through professional conduct and business practices.

To divert focus for a moment and look abroad, consider the origins of the founder of the Rothschild financial empire. Mayer Amschel Rothschild grew up in the Judengasse Jewish quarters of Frankfurt in Germany in a large family with many siblings; so, finding talent and managers for the business was rarely a problem in the early years. The rigorous conditions of Rothschild's upbringing in a ghetto and a good head for numbers were certainly positive factors in his future success as a banker, as were his go-getting nature and his readiness to build connections rather than make immediate profits. Both these qualities suggest that his long-term outlook for business weighed in on his decision making. He conceded, like few business people do, that luck played a role in success. But for him, luck was not some random event. The recipient of luck had to be prepared to spot and seize any happy chance.[4]

The elements of Rothschild's success, except for his extensive family and the hardships of Judengasse, apply to Uday Kotak as well. Kotak in fact ejected himself from a readymade driver's seat in the family's traditional business of cotton and textiles, let alone use his family for employment in the bank. Kotak was, and singularly is, focused on capability-building to grow his bank. The narrative of this book explains his keen eye for people as much as his sharp nose for smelling opportunity and his clear head for numbers.

We hope this book about Kotak Mahindra Bank enthuses and highlights the principles of 'The Kotak Way' with facts and rich anecdotes. Caution requires that Kotak Mahindra Bank not yet be declared among India's finest business institutions, but the potential for such an event is high. While there has been some concern over what would happen after Uday Kotak, we were reassured that the institution has in place a robust succession plan. There are systems, processes, protocols and a deeply-rooted culture that have been built since the mid-'80s to help the bank survive across generations, as desired by Uday as well.

The future beckons, with all its uncertainties and challenges. Led by Uday, Kotak Mahindra Bank has adroitly, yet miraculously survived crisis after crisis and in doing so, may well have patched this survival gene into its DNA. After all, to be counted as one of the fastest growing banks and most admired financial institutions in India is no mean feat.[5]

---

[4]Landes, David S. *Dynasties: Fortunes and Misfortunes of the World's Greatest Business Families*. Viking, 2006.
[5]'Kotak Mahindra Bank Reports'. *NDTV*, https://www.ndtv.com/business/stock/kotak-mahindra-bank-ltd_kotakbank/report. Accessed 4 July 2020.

# Chapter 1

# Of Uncertainty, Chaos and Repression

*Do not go where the path may lead, go instead where there is no path and leave a trail.*

—Ralph Waldo Emerson

Bombay[1], 1982. It was the City of Dreams, with its heady mix of Bollywood and business—luring into its swirling vortex all those unsuspecting millions who possessed an entrepreneurial streak—the promise of opportunities and the possibility of making untold wealth. Uday Kotak,[2] a 23-year-old management graduate from Jamnalal Bajaj Institute of Management Studies (JBIMS), one of the most prestigious business schools of the city, succumbed to the city's charms and broke away from his family-owned and managed business in cotton and textiles to venture out on his own. His entrepreneurial journey is an astounding one in terms

---

[1]Bombay was renamed Mumbai in 1995. Both names have been used interchangeably in the text.
[2]While Uday Kotak is referred to as Uday in the book, Kotak refers to Uday's company Kotak Mahindra Finance Ltd. (KMFL) or Kotak Mahindra Bank or its subsidiaries.

of sheer audacity, ability to think out of the box and spot opportunities yet unperceived to create history and one of India's most valuable and trusted banks within a short span of less than two decades.

This success would have been difficult to foresee, considering the business environment and financial landscape prevailing in India at the time was not conducive to warrant such 'fool-hardy' behaviour of throwing away a secure career to step into another one plagued with risk and uncertainty. India, through much of the '80s and indeed for decades prior to it, had been riddled by an economic system which concentrated more on what one could *not* do, rather than what one *could* do. And yet a shaper, with a mindset to break barriers, is one who actually flourishes in such an environment by identifying and circumventing the obstacles with a clear determination and focus, which in turn becomes one of his most potent weapons. The first step in understanding this mindset is to understand the nature of such barriers and the backdrop within which the 'shaper' mindset was born. This context itself was shaped largely by the political circumstances of the day, which is what we turn to next.

## INDIA DURING INDIRA

India had witnessed a long period of politics dominated by a single, powerful leader up until the 1970s. The slogan 'India is Indira and Indira is India' coined by Dev Kant Barooah, who served as President of the Indian National Congress between 1975-77, speaks of the hold that a strong political class and its supporters had had over India's fortunes. The socialistic pattern of development that India had chosen for itself post-

Independence ensured the primacy of political influence in its development story. The Second Five Year Plan, based on the Mahalanobis development strategy promoted government-led industrialization that set into motion an upward spiral of increasing influence. The then Prime Minister Jawaharlal Nehru's statement, 'The public sector must grow not only absolutely, but also relatively to the private sector,' captures the sentiment of the period.

With politicians suspecting businesses of being corrupt and exploitative, those in power chose to shackle private enterprise in a complex system of licenses, regulations and bureaucracy. The system, pejoratively termed 'License Raj,' was one where the government used a conditional system of licenses to approve or reject all private-business related decisions, ranging from which company could produce goods, in what quantities, where they could do so and the price at which they could sell. Company boards had no role in such a scenario.

While License Raj stifled private entrepreneurs and businesses, it also meant a regime of scarcity for consumers, who had to make do with sub-standard, second-grade products in limited numbers, be it cars or jeans. The licenses themselves being a scarce commodity, were traded in markets at corresponding prices. There were instances where licenses were acquired to pre-empt competition and not necessarily to enter production—this despite the dreaded Monopolies and Restrictive Trade Practices (MRTP) Act of 1970. Industrialist Dhirubai Ambani is quoted as having said that the art of managing government relationships was most critical to business success[3].

---

[3]Neeraj Agarwal. 'India before 1991: Stories of life under the License Raj.'

The system of licenses and controls was extended to regulate imports as well and right up to the late 1970s, the Indian economy was characterized by a system of repressive import controls. With high import tariffs, bans and quotas, Indian consumers could not exercise their choice to buy, even if they had the purchasing power to do so.

## TELEVISION CONSUMERISM

Even as the economy continued to remain shackled, a new medium of communication enabled Indian consumers to see and hear of products and services which they could not access. The television (TV)—introduced pan-India in the 1980s—was itself the result of a slow, but perceptible change in the Indian mindset. When it was first brought to Delhi in September 1959 with the help of the United Nations Educational, Scientific and Cultural Organization (UNESCO), the TV was frowned upon by Indian policy makers as a luxury. The content and duration of TV-viewing was restricted by the government, probably with the intent of saving the 'naïve' natives from being corrupted. One TV channel—Doordarshan—was allowed to broadcast twice a week for an hour a day, on social themes such as community health, traffic and road sense, citizens' duties and rights, etc.

For nearly two decades since the introduction of television, India and Indians had to contend with the unimaginative black and white TV and watching TV was usually a community affair. It was only in 1982, when India hosted the Asian

---

*Spontaneous Order*, 30 March 2016, https://spontaneousorder.in/india-before-91/. Accessed 4 July 2020.

Games and the government introduced colour broadcasts of the Games, that TV actually spread its wings. When Indians bought 'personal' TVs for their houses, Doordarshan was able to reach 90 per cent of India's population through a network of nearly 1400 terrestrial transmitters,[4] with novel content including song clips from Bollywood films (1982) and family oriented soaps (1986-87) and mythological dramas (1987-89) created especially for Indian viewers.

Television also meant that the political leadership could use the single available channel—Doordarshan—to influence hundreds of millions of citizens with a uniform message. People who watched TV had suddenly come to aspire for goods and services that were being streamed into their living rooms every day—a consumerist culture was being slowly unleashed.[5] A new breed of worshippers of Mammon was being created, with consequences extending into the financial sector.

## REFORMS FOR THE 21ST CENTURY

The idea of a single leader was challenged briefly in the 1970s. The 21-month Emergency imposed across India between June 1975 to March 1977, culminated in the general elections that were contested on the plank of the Emergency experience. The opposition parties in India 'united' under one umbrella, under Jayaprakash Narayan, to form the Janata Party that became the first non-Congress party to win the general elections, with a

---

[4]*Press Information Bureau*, pib.gov.in/newsite/printrelease.aspx?relid =169686. Accessed 4 July 2020.
[5]'India In The 1980s: The Lull That Shaped the Storm.' *Forbes India*, 12 August 2019, www.forbesindia.com/article/independence-special-2019/india-in-the-1980s-the-lull-that-shaped-the-storm/54779/1. Accessed 4 July 2020.

thumping majority. Yet it only stayed in power between 1977 and 1980 and blew its chance to provide a viable alternative to Indira, through their infighting and lack of governance.

The election results of the seventh general elections, held in India in 1980, unsurprisingly, returned Indira to her third term of prime ministership, with a clean sweep of 353 Lok Sabha seats.

However, the Indian political landscape was about to witness upheaval, as the lotus bloomed for the first time, with the establishment of the Bharatiya Janata Party (BJP) in April 1980. Sanjay Gandhi, Indira Gandhi's anointed successor, was killed in an air-crash in June 1980.[6] A distraught Mrs Gandhi continued stoically and four years later, in 1984, ordered one of the largest internal military operations ever undertaken by the Indian Army—Operation Blue Star, that stormed the Golden Temple in Amritsar—to restore law and order in Punjab leading to widespread anguish and resentment among Sikhs worldwide. Widely perceived as retaliation for Operation Blue Star, Mrs Gandhi was assassinated by her two Sikh bodyguards on 31 October 1984.[7]

Her elder son, Rajiv Gandhi, who had been drafted into a political career after his brother's death, was sworn in as prime minister on the same day and helmed the landslide

---

[6]'Sanjay Gandhi Dies in a Dramatic Plane Crash, His Passing to Leave a Political Vacuum.' *India Today*, 2 December 2014, www.indiatoday.in/magazine/cover-story/story/19800715-sanjay-gandhi-dies-in-a-dramatic-plane-crash-his-passing-to-leave-a-political-vacuum-821253-2014-01-22. Accessed 4 July 2020.

[7]'What Happened During 1984 Operation Blue Star?' *India Today*, 6 June 2018, www.indiatoday.in/fyi/story/1984-operation-blue-star-amritsar-1251681-2018-06-06. Accessed 4 July 2020.

victory of the Congress in the Lok Sabha elections held in December 1984. He is credited with introducing measures to liberalize the Indian economy and reform the government bureaucracy.[8]

Historically weighed down by a 'low level GDP growth baggage', India's average growth rate over the entire 10-year period from 1978-79 to 1987-88 was a mere 4.1 per cent. However, its year-by-year growth rates revealed the picture of a remarkably fast-growing country in certain years. While India achieved a 10.5 per cent growth rate in 1988-89, it grew at an equally rapid pace during the next three-year period, 1989-91, driven by a culture of consumerism, fuelled by the images beamed into Indian homes through the TV. Such consumerism was given further fillip with Rajiv taking on the political mantle.

## LIBERALIZATION BY STEALTH

Aided by his young, Western-oriented, 'no-nonsense' team,[9] Rajiv initiated the 'liberalization' of India, firing up the country's imagination by allowing them to dream of a future where consumption and profit were not taboo.[10]

---

[8]'Rajiv Gandhi.' *Encyclopedia Britannica*, www.britannica.com/biography/Rajiv-Gandhi. Accessed 4 July 2020.

[9]His team included V.P. Singh (finance minister), Sam Pitroda (technocrat), Montek Singh Ahluwalia (economist)and V. Krishnamurthy (regarded as the doyen of the public sector).

[10]'In an India Known for Thinking Small, Rajiv Gandhi Generated High-stakes Optimism.' *India Today*, 11 September 2013, www.indiatoday.in/magazine/cover-story/story/19910615-in-an-india-known-for-thinking-small-rajiv-gandhi-generated-high-stakes-optimism-814461-1991-06-15. Accessed 4 July 2020.

While these efforts were never referred to as liberalization or reforms, India experienced 'liberalization by stealth'[11] much before the introduction of the historic 1991 reforms, known by the acronym *LPG*—Liberalization, Privatization and Globalization, which helped Indian industry grow at an average rate of 9.2 per cent during 1989-91.

The Rajiv government substantially relaxed the earlier import controls[12] and gave up the exclusive monopoly rights it had held over imports of certain items. The freeing up of these essential imports immediately led to a significant increase in India's productivity as exports too opened up and exporters were provided key incentives. Post 1984, certain provisions of the dreaded License Raj—seen as stifling competition and restricting productivity and growth—were wound up or relaxed. By 1990, 31 industries were de-licensed. Investment limits for industrial licensing were substantially relaxed as were provisions of the MRTP Act. Under V.P. Singh as finance minister, the government also simplified the tax system and lowered the rate of taxation.[13]

Though termed 'complex and arbitrary',[14] these reforms significantly accelerated the industrial growth rate to 9.2 per cent from 1988 to 1991, which was relatively high compared to

---

[11]A. Panagriya. 'India in the 1980s and 1990s: A Triumph of reforms.' *IMF Working* Paper, 2004, WP/04/43https://www.imf.org/external/pubs/ft/wp/2004/wp0443.pdf. Accessed 4 July 2020.

[12]Unfortunately, these reforms suffered a setback after the breaking of the Bofors scandal in 1987.

[13]'A Chronology of Income Tax Since 1950s.' *India Today*, 26 February 2010, www.indiatoday.in/business/budget/story/a-chronology-of-income-tax-since-1950s-67424-2010-02-15. Accessed 4 July 2020.

[14]Ashok Desai.'The Economics and Politics of Transition to an Open Market Economy: India.' *OECD Working Papers*, Volume VII, No. 100, 1999, p. 21.

earlier periods as well as to other developing economies at the time. India experienced this growth even in the clear absence of a well-developed financial system, comprising banks and financial intermediaries to facilitate the mobilization of capital for large-scale investments, usually a pre-requisite for growth.

## OF GROWTH AND FINANCIAL REPRESSION

For the government, regulation of the financial sector held the key to keeping the industry and the economy under control. This was also warranted by the socialistic model of development that India had chosen for itself at the time of commencement of its Five-Year Plans. The 'financial repression' of India's banks and other financial intermediaries was thus evidenced on multiple fronts—whether it was the government's systematic take-over of the banking sector by nationalizing all banks, an ad hoc system of administered interest rates, the system of directing and micro-regulating the flow of credit lending to particular sectors and regions or even the large pre-emption of banking sector deposits by the government.

Yet, in spite of government intervention, private bank branches grew at a far more rapid pace than those of public sector banks between 1969 and 1980. On 1 April 1980, private bank branches accounted for approximately 17.5 per cent of bank branches in India. These banks, the government felt, suffered from governance problems. Moreover, the problem of credit delivery had to be addressed as well. A worried government then undertook another round of nationalization in April 1980 and placed six private banks, accounting for 8 per cent of bank branches and with nationwide deposits above ₹2 billion, under government control.[15] At the time, only 10 per cent of bank branches were in private hands.[16] Such banks were used for 'loan melas', essentially a means of distributing unsecured loans at subsidized interest rates largely to the rural poor and to preferred industrialists.[17]

While controlling the banking sector aided in controlling the quantity of money disbursed in the economy, financial sector repression also involved control over interest rates— the price of finance—through what was called a system of Administered Interest Rates. Since October 1958, interest rates in India were not determined by market forces of demand and supply of funds. Rather, the government began to fix interest rates either through fiat or through discretionary administrative controls that extended to all kinds of interest rates,[18] which were moreover changed haphazardly and in an ad hoc manner.

The government kept all these interest rates artificially lower—justifying them on the basis of the needs of a developing country.[19] For instance, up to 1981-82, the yield

---

[15]The six banks nationalized at this stage were: Andhra Bank, Corporation Bank, New Bank of India, Oriental Bank of Commerce, Punjab and Sind Bank and Vijaya Bank.

[16]Banerjee, A. V., Cole, S., & Duflo, E. (2004). *Banking Reform in India*. https://economics.mit.edu/files/16602. Accessed 4 July 2020.

[17]'India in The 1980s: The Lull that Shaped the Storm.' *Forbes India*, 12 Aug. 2019, www.forbesindia.com/article/independence-special-2019/india-in-the-1980s-the-lull-that-shaped-the-storm/54779/1. Accessed 4 July 2020.

[18]The government-controlled Interest rates on deposit and lending rates of commercial banks, co-operative banks, postal savings organizations, non-banking companies and the lending rates of term-lending financial institutions.

[19]Bhole, L.M. 'Administered Interest rates in India.' *Economic & Political Weekly*, Vol. 20, No. 25/26, 1985, pp.1089-1104.

on government securities, considered the gold standard among securities, was lower than the interest rate paid by banks on deposits of one to three years maturity. Similarly, the spread between the interest rates at which the banks collected funds through deposits and the rates at which the banks lent their funds tended to be large. By 1985, this spread differential between bank deposit and lending rates was 10 per cent or more, creating opportunities for arbitrage wherein Uday spotted his first business break. With the government announcing different types and rates of interest, the system was extremely 'complex and unmanageable.'[20] The government further controlled such finance by setting ceilings on the amount of credit that could be distributed to different borrowers, sectors, uses, etc.

Another area of exercising control was through Priority Sector Lending (PSL) programme, identified as one of the longest serving directed lending programmes in the world. The government in 1968 identified a set of sectors which were important and in line with the national economic policy. These 'priority' sectors initially comprised agriculture and small-scale industries. Commercial banks were asked to increase their involvement in the financing of these sectors. In 1980, priority sector lending was also made applicable to private sector banks and all banks—private and public—were asked to raise the level of advances to the priority sector to 40 per cent by March 1985. Sub-targets were also specified for lending to agriculture and the weaker sections within the priority sector.[21]

---

[20]Ibid., p.1094.
[21]'Reports.' *Reserve Bank of India*, www.rbi.org.in/Scripts/Publication

Bank funds were also pre-empted in a manner that prevented them from using all the deposits they had mopped up in the best possible manner. The government used two channels to pre-empt bank funds—the Cash Reserve Ratio (CRR) and the Statutory Liquidity Ratio (SLR). The CRR was the percentage share of a bank's total deposits mandated to be maintained as cash deposits in its books with the RBI. This meant that with a CRR of 15 per cent as in 1989, the bank could lend to businesses out of only 85 per cent of its total deposits. The RBI paid no interest on these cash deposits; however, failure to maintain CRR could attract a penalty from the RBI.[22] An additional CRR of 10 per cent was introduced effective 1983, which further reduced the lendable resources.

Additionally, the bank also had to keep aside another portion of its deposits as the SLR,[23] in the form of cash, gold or investments in short and long-term government securities, *with itself.* The RBI could impose a penal rate of interest,

---

ReportDetails.aspx?ID=810.; http://www.iibf.org.in/documents/reseachreport/Macro_Research_Rethinking_PSL_Final_Report.pdf; 'Priority Sector Lending (PSL)'. Arthapedia, www.arthapedia.in/index.php?title=Priority_Sector_Lending. Accessed 4 July 2020.

[22]Kanagasabapathy, K. 'CRR and SLR in Indian Banking'. *The Hindu Businessline*, 25 Oct. 2012, www.thehindubusinessline.com/opinion/columns/k-kanagasabapathy/crr-and-slr-in-indian-banking/article22986055.ece; 'Chronology of Events'. *Reserve Bank of India*, www.rbi.org.in/scripts/chro_bankrate.aspx; 'Cash Reserve Ratio (CRR)'. *Arthapedia*, www.arthapedia.in/index.php?title=Cash_Reserve_Ratio_(CRR). Accessed 4 July 2020.

[23]The SLR had to be maintained under the Banking Regulation Act 1949. The SLR, which was at 20 per cent when it was introduced in 1949, rose to 34 per cent in 1978 and 38.5 per cent in 1990. Such SLR provided the government a captive market for its securities and implied no risks in refinancing were it to be faced by a debt crisis. The government borrowed at low, administered interest rates.

and other penalty in case banks failed to comply with the SLR requirements.[24] With the SLR at 38 per cent as in 1989, commercial banks would have to keep aside 38 per cent, 15 per cent and 10 per cent—totalling 63 per cent of its total deposits for SLR and CRR respectively—and hence would have only 37 per cent of its deposits available for lending. Further requirements of priority sector lending meant that banks could lend no more than 40 per cent of their overall deposits in a competitive manner to business and industry.[25]

It is in the context of such financial repression and growth that the making of our shaper and his impact on the organization, operating within the peculiarities of the Indian financial sector, need to be understood. Even when a more liberal trading climate in the mid- '80s benefitted traders and entrepreneurs like the Kotak family, Uday chose to turn his back on a readymade business and decided instead, to enter the financial sector, which faced increasing repression at the time.

The growth in the mid-1980s, when Uday entered India's financial sector, though higher than the earlier periods, was extremely 'fragile', financed as it was, by government borrowing and spending beyond its means, that led to inflation. The government then sought to curb inflation

---

[24]'Chronology Of Events.' *Reserve Bank of India*, www.rbi.org.in/scripts/chro_bankrate.aspx; 'Statutory Liquidity Ratio.' Arthapedia, www.arthapedia.in/index.php?title=Statutory_Liquidity_Ratio.

[25]Jose, Tojo. 'What is Double Financial Repression?' *Indian Economy*, 2 Feb. 2016, www.indianeconomy.net/splclassroom/what-is-double-financial-repression/; Accessed 4 July 2020.

The RBI notes this as well. 'Thus, by 1991, 63.5 per cent resources of the banking sector were pre-empted in the form of SLR and CRR.' 'Publications.' *Reserve Bank of India*, www.rbi.org.in/scripts/publicationsview.aspx?id=10487.

through administered and regulated interest rates, pre-empting bank funds through high reserve requirements and credit rationing, effectively preventing the development of financial markets.[26]

It was in such a market, where liberalization on the external and domestic front was matched with severe financial repression, that a young man from an Indian business family entered the Indian financial services sector. Was it the sheer romanticism of youth that led Uday to chart a path for himself in an undeniably difficult industry? We explore the mindset which led him to do this, as we unravel the fascinating journey of the Shaper and the Institution that he built, in the following chapters.

---

[26]Mohan, R. 'India's Financial sector reforms: Fostering growth while containing risk.' *BIS Review*, 2007, https://www.bis.org/review/r071207e.pdf. Accessed 4 July 2020.

# Chapter 2

# An Entrepreneur is Born

'Whether you think you can, or think
you can't—you're right.'

—Henry Ford, Founder Ford Motors

Karachi, Pre-Partition India. A Gujarati trading family originally from Rajkot, that had served the erstwhile ruler of Rajkot state, Lakhajiraj, set up a company for trading in cotton. Kotak & Co., registered in Bombay in 1927, was a family business, run by Amritlal Kotak and his five brothers. While Amritlal handled the business from Karachi, his brothers spread out across other parts of the world, including Bombay, Shanghai and Japan. The demand for cotton was high and the business was profitable as Karachi was the main trading centre and an important port of undivided India.

Amritlal, and indeed the entire family, was influenced by Gandhiji and Gandhian principles of simple living and high thinking, with strong ethical values and a keen sense of social responsibility. Suresh Kotak, Amritlal's eldest son, born in 1933, had his early education in Sharada Mandir, a Gandhian school in Karachi. Having been a volunteer when Gandhiji had visited Karachi, Suresh went on to participate in the nationalist movement.[27]

In 1946, however, the spectre of Partition began to loom large. Karachi had become too risky for life and trade. Amritlal decided to shift with his family to Bombay, where he already had extended family staying and carrying on the family business of cotton trade. In 1947, his wife, Suresh and three children—Taruna, Usha and Sudhir—shifted to Bombay. It was almost as if they were refugees; they were given a small corner of the house at Babul Nath, near Chowpatty. Amritlal also migrated to India shortly and joined the main branch of the family business. Suresh completed his graduation from Sydenham College of Commerce & Economics and entered the family business of cotton trade, despite his own dreams of going to the US for higher education. At the age of 25, Suresh was married to Indira, the 20-year-old daughter of another well-known Gujarati, realtor and contractor Devkaran Nenshi Tanna, whose firm is known for building the Marine Drive, a Mumbai landmark.

## EARLY LESSONS

As was common among Indian business families, especially those belonging to the early independence era, the entire family, comprising of 63 family members, lived together under one roof—a huge floor in a large house—and shared one kitchen. In this home and into a well-off, but conservative and traditional Gujarati business family, Uday was born to

---

[27]The Nationalist Movements in India (1885-1919) were organized mass movements that fostered patriotism and raised questions about the interests of the people of India and foreign domination over it by England.

Suresh and Indira on 15 March 1959. The entire family, especially Amritlal and his wife, were overjoyed at the birth of a grandchild and Uday was the apple of their eye. As Suresh reminisces, 'My father was so fond of Uday that he would not have his lunch or dinner without him.'

In 1963, a new school was set up in Marine Lines. The school, Hindi Vidya Bhavan, was inaugurated by Morarji Desai, a Gandhian and an activist of the Independence Movement. The school sought to promote international-level English-medium education steeped in Indian values. Despite the fact that the children of this business family could have studied in any of the better-known and recognized schools of Bombay at the time, like Campion School or Cathedral School, one of the elders of the family decided that they would go to a school that promised nationalist ideals. And so, the children, one or two years apart, were all sent to Hindi Vidya Bhavan. As Uday puts it, 'I believe that a joint family business is a classic case of capitalism at work and socialism within the family and at home. That was the basis of growing up in that family house.'

As the family grew, Amritlal felt the need to move due to the constraints of space. So, when Uday was about four years old, Amritlal moved to a separate house on Laburnum Road in Gamdevi South Bombay with his wife, children and grandchildren, to set up their 'independent' family. The new home was opposite Mani Bhavan,[28] Gandhiji's Bombay headquarters for 17 years. When Uday's uncle, Sudhir got

[28]Mani Bhavan, the focal point of Mahatma Gandhi's political activities in Mumbai between 1917 and 1934, is a museum today; a historical building dedicated to Gandhi.

married, the 'satellite' family comprised 10 members, a significant reduction from the earlier number of 63, and yet a 'joint family' by any standards. The family continued to deal in cotton. By the late 1960s however, the business was diversified into yarn, cotton waste and agri-commodities.

Living within a business family, young Uday received some early lessons in different leadership styles. His father, Suresh was responsible for sourcing cotton from far-flung markets in Bhatinda, Punjab, Hissar, Haryana and Sri Ganganagar, Rajasthan—all cotton-growing centres. In those days without mobile telephony, a trader would have to rely entirely on landlines to carry on his business, using phone calls to buy cotton and then to sell it further. The telecom authority regulations of the day meant that any landline calls placed before 6 a.m. were charged at half the price. So, Suresh would wake up early in the morning, just like his father, and his first task of the day was to book trunk calls to up-country markets and clients. Suresh would also speak to his agent in Coimbatore, Tamil Nadu, where the mills were located, and would buy and sell cotton.

When Uday would wake up around 7:30 a.m., he would find Suresh and Amritlal sitting across each other, engrossed in business discussions. The discussions would centre largely around the prices of cotton in the mandis[29] and the demand in the mills in Coimbatore. A six- or seven-year old Uday would climb onto his grandfather's lap. He remembers how, perched on his grandfather's lap, even at that age, he was able to perceive the differences in style and approach between his father and grandfather.

---

[29]Mandi refers to the market place, usually commodity specific.

Looking back on those days, Uday recalls a typical dialogue between the two. He said,

My grandfather has lived through the Great Depression era of the 1930s. Born in 1906, his youth spent during the Depression made him extremely conservative, detail-oriented and focused on the full-cost model. So, when buying cotton from the mandi, he would estimate all input costs like fixed overheads and some profit before arriving at the sales price for the mill.

My father, on the other hand, was a big picture guy. He would say, you don't need to do full costing. Once in a while, we can make a sale on marginal costing to ensure we cover the fixed costs. My grandfather would say that is the wrong approach for business and that it would hurt us over time.

For many years, I observed such debates between them; on what price to sell at, what price to buy at, how to conserve, what costing to consider. What I consider a great learning in my formative years is my grandfather's attention to detail. He would often tell me and my father as well, '*Beta, tumne 1930 ki mandhi nahi dekhi. Dus saal chali thi.* (Son, you haven't seen the economic recession of the 1930s. It lasted 10 years).'

My grandfather lived frugally. He would wear a traditional khadi or linen half kurta that was not discarded even when it tore. He would stitch it and wear it. When we questioned him, he would advise us: '*Paisa waste mat karo. Maine tees ki mandhi dekhi hai* (Don't waste money. I have seen the recession of the '30s).'

Uday respects and values these cultural imprints, deeply

ingrained within him, especially in present times.

On being questioned about Amritlal being his role model, as reflected in his own legendary detail-orientedness, Uday displays the characteristic Shaper trait of *Critical Thinking*, a mindset that enables one to consider multiple options and objectively evaluate the pros and cons of each. This mindset translates into behaviour that encourages discussion and debate with open-mindedness. Thus, while his grandfather's approach impressed Uday, he was able to see the merit in his father's macro-view argument as well. He states, 'My father would always argue with my grandfather, saying, "You are wrong. These are inflationary times; there is a high fiscal deficit, a weakening rupee. Therefore, think inflationary, do not think deflationary."'

From a young age, Uday was able to absorb multiple perspectives. While his father's perspective geared him to look at the macro picture, his grandfather's view trained him to assess the granular details. In fact, he states that one of the most critical aspects of their business is the ability to think big picture and granular simultaneously. He explains, 'There are times where you have to let details go and then there are times where you focus on the strategic direction, even if there are costs to be borne. So, keeping the balance is often a difficult judgement call.'

This practice of weighing multiple perspectives is useful in making important business decisions. As Uday candidly admits, he would put himself into his father as well as his grandfather's shoes and think of how each one would debate the issue at hand, before taking critical business decisions.

Another set of early lessons Uday imbibed from his grandfather were related to monitoring risk and risk management. From Amritlal, a visionary and shrewd business man, he would learn how to minimize expenses, how not to spend on anything wasteful and how to run a business—all of which he lapped up since childhood. Suresh acknowledges that the deepest influences on Uday were his grandfather and mother. Amritlal, in fact, continued to be Uday's sounding board and counsel until his death in 1994.

## FAMILY VALUES

The Kotak family's deep sense of values is embedded in Gandhian principles. One of Amritlal's brothers was a nationalist, a Gandhian and close to Morarji Desai. Uday's father, Suresh, an octogenarian today, is hailed by his peers as the 'Cotton Man of India.' He is known for his association with multiple causes, especially social initiatives and research in cotton. Suresh has played an important role in various educational institutions in Rajkot, the place from where the family originally hails. He says, 'I believe in education for the growth and development of people. Education should be skill-based; it should help people earn a livelihood.'

Suresh does not mince his words on what he thinks is the *dharma* of family businesses. He believes, 'A family business should not be the preserve of a family; it should be *a reserve of the society.*' Similar thoughts come through in our discussions with Uday as well and it is not difficult to glean the source of such an influence.

The Kotak family's fundamental philosophy, 'Provide enough for everyone's need, but not enough for everyone's greed,' was reflected in the children's upbringing. For instance, Uday would go to school by bus with none of the frills and comfort of being driven to school in the family car, as was common among upper-class Indian families. However, when the other children of the family also reached school-going age, the family sent them all in a single car to Hindi Vidya Bhavan. Just like the transition from school bus to car, all decisions in the family were influenced by a sense of thrift.

Even when Uday enrolled into Sydenham College of Commerce and Economics for his graduate studies, he would board the bus from just outside Laburnum Road, which would take him to Natraj Hotel, near Churchgate. Sydenham College was just a stone's throw away from there. 'The bus ticket cost just five paisa initially,' Uday recollects with amusement. 'We were perfectly comfortable with this simple middle-class ethos,' he quips. Uday believes that irrespective of availability of finances, it is upon the family to provide children a firm mooring in values with a higher sense of value for money.

## THE FEMININE INFLUENCE

While the men in the family had a deep influence on Uday, the role of the women—especially his mother and grandmother—as he was growing up, was equally important. Suresh speaks of his wife, Indira, with great pride. She was a brilliant student of science and he attributes much of Uday's personality traits to his mother.

Suresh says, with utmost modesty,

Of course, I have influenced him on the business front. But as far as his character development is concerned, his mother and grandfather have played a dominant role.

Uday's sister, Aarti, was born eight years after him. So Uday received his mother's undivided attention for most of his growing up years. In fact, Indira had completely thrown herself into Uday's development and education.

While the nights would be spent on a mattress on the floor, safely tucked in his grandparent's room, Uday fondly remembers how food played a crucial part in his relationship with his mother. Like most Indian mothers, Indira would insist on coming to Uday's school with his tiffin during lunch time. She was skilled at mathematics, particularly algebra and geometry, and tutored Uday through class seven to 10. In fact, he seems to have inherited his mother's flair for mathematics, a love-affair with numbers that would determine the course of his life.

Indira's attention and loving care for the child yielded results early. Uday was an orator par excellence, stood out in studies, sport and arts and thus, was extremely versatile. Suresh recounts how Uday, a member of the Interact club[30] in school, was invited to speak at the District Rotary Club. He was just 13 then, and the youngest speaker at the event that was graced by General Sam Maneckshaw, the Commander-In-Chief of the Indian Army, as the chief guest. As Suresh recalls, 'Uday's speech, related to the social aspects and duties of Interact, was a remarkable exposition of social values.' That this is not just a proud father speaking about his son is evident from General Maneckshaw's reaction to the young boy. The

---

[30]Interact is the Rotary-sponsored service club for youngsters, in the age group typically of 14-18. Interact gives young people an opportunity to participate in fun, yet meaningful service projects. Along the way, Interactors develop their leadership skills and initiative while meeting new friends.

general had hugged him, even as Uday received a standing ovation from the audience.

Indira was a huge pillar of support for Uday. Even as a child, he was highly competitive and would hate coming second in anything. He would be upset if he lost the first position and would make his mother his sounding board, quarrelling with her and asking her why he deserved this. As Suresh recalls, 'Indira would say, what more can I do? I am dancing with you.'

Much like his mother, Uday never gave up and adapted quickly to situations. For instance, while still in lower kindergarten, his teacher complained to his mother, 'Your boy is useless. He can't even write.' Indira was perplexed and protested, 'At home he writes everything.' They finally figured out that Uday was left-handed, whereas in school, the teacher was trying to get him to write using his right hand.

Uday confirmed that he is a left-hander, even though while eating, he holds the fork in his right hand. Uday explained this seeming inconsistency with a twinkle in his eyes, 'That's because you are forced to, you have been trained to do this,' before letting us into a little secret, 'When I play cricket, I am a right-hand batsman, but a left-hand spinner.'

Uday was an avid cricket player and could have possibly even led the National XI. Cricket was certainly on the cards as a career choice, as was the family business, until one day, within a moment, life, as he knew it, changed. It is Uday's penchant to adapt quickly and ambidextrously play the balls that life throws at him, with focus and determination, keeping the big picture in mind. This ability built the man we call the Shaper, and the organization we call one of our six 'Institutions', as we shall see in the next chapter.

# Chapter 3

# In Search of Destiny

'The only person you are destined to become is
the person you decide to be.'

—Ralph Waldo Emerson

Uday's presence in the Indian banking industry owes a debt to destiny. If fate had not intervened, India would probably have had a brilliant right-hand batsman and left-hand spinner. India's loss is a gain for the corporate world.

Notwithstanding Uday's early struggle to keep up with one of the 3R's—Reading, Writing and Arithmetic—he completed his school years as an above-average student, always among the top three. In his first year at Sydenham College of Commerce and Economics, a revered institution affiliated to Bombay University, he stood second in the university—a feat that 'stunned' him and 'acted as a big spur'. The desire to excel in studies motivated him and he went on to top the university, both at the Junior B.Com. and B.Com. levels. After graduation, faced with a choice to either pursue Chartered Accountancy or a Masters in Business Administration (MBA), he made up his mind when Jamnalal Bajaj Institute of Management Studies (JBIMS) offered him a seat in its prestigious two-year MBA programme. He pursued the MBA, even as he followed his twin passions of cricket and sitar.

## PLAYING THE GENTLEMAN'S GAME

Cricket, in particular, was more than just a passing interest. He was an ace batsman, who played the game passionately. He had already captained the cricket team both at Hindi Vidya Bhavan and at Sydenham College. Coach Ramakant Achrekar, who was later cricket icon Sachin Tendulkar's coach too, recollects the cricket practice sessions when Uday used to captain the Hindi Vidya Bhavan school team. Achrekar would summon the best bowler on the team and challenge him to knock off Kotak's middle stump. If everything had worked out as planned, Uday would have probably liked to play cricket for the country, but it was not to be.

It was September 1979. Uday had just joined the first year of MBA at JBIMS. His passion for cricket drew him to Azad Maidan to play a Kanga League match, which is part of Mumbai's rich cricketing lore and which unwittingly contributed to the shaping of the banker.

The Kanga League holds a certain romance in the mind of every cricket-loving Mumbaikar, and was the gold standard for aspiring cricketers long before the Indian Premier League and its Mumbai Indians became popular. Started in 1948 by Vijay Merchant, a famous yester-year's cricketer, the tournament aimed to prepare Indians to beat the English at their own game, quite literally, by simulating English weather conditions during the monsoon months in Mumbai and making Indian cricketers play on an uncovered wicket.

As the only monsoon cricket tournament in the world, the League offered one of the toughest conditions for batsmen, where 'the ball could stop, shoot, skid and swing—all in a day's play',[31] depending on the conditions in the sky. Playing conditions were tough, as bowlers needed to circumvent puddles in their run-up, fielders and umpires would have mud splashing on their faces when the ball bounced in front of them and the nature of the pitch changed by the hour. A rain-break meant that players were forced to retreat into their tents, sip some hot tea with biscuits and wait for play to resume. Yet, the Kanga League represented the grassroots legacy of Mumbai cricket.

The Kanga League not only provided Bombay the culture of competitive cricket, but playing under difficult monsoon conditions gave players from the city a 'head start in national tournaments', as articulated by Milind Rege, a former Mumbai captain, making them the strongest side in Indian cricket, practicing 'khadoos'[32] batting as it were. In fact, the League became so important that Mumbai selectors picked Ranji Trophy players from these tournaments.

Playing fast and hard had its drawbacks too. Playing on an uncovered wicket meant the possibility of major physical

---

[31]Puthran, Ayush. 'The Romance and Relevance of Kanga League Cricket.' *Cricbuzz*, 6 August 2016, m.cricbuzz.com/cricket-news/81889/spotlight-the-romance-and-relevance-of-kanga-league-cricket-by-aayush-puthran. Accessed 4 July 2020.

[32]Austin Coutinho, a former Kanga League pacer said, 'We call them [Mumbai batsmen] 'khadoos' (rude, snobbish and uncaring for others) because they used to go and bat on absolutely horrible drying wickets. Playing in those conditions is not only about the technique, it is also about the mental aspect. When you are going to bat on such wickets, you are ready to face whatever comes. You get tough mentally.'

harm, as attested by cricketer Madhav Apte,[33] who said, 'We have all played, right up to Sunil Gavaskar, fast bowling under all kinds of conditions and without any protective gear, without helmets and no regulation on bouncers. Without the comfort of protection, with high possibility of injury, batsmen were more alert and watching the ball more closely.'

## A Serious Setback

It was when Uday was playing under such conditions, on a balmy Sunday morning that the unthinkable happened. Uday flicked a shot between the covers and as he was running between the wickets, a fielder flung the ball back to the stumps in order to get him run out. The ball hit Uday on the head and he collapsed. He doesn't remember how all of it happened, but the competitive spirit in him prevailed. He got up and continued to play till the end of the game, for another half an hour. His head hurt and his team mates wanted to take him to the hospital but Uday insisted on being taken home. His friends bundled him into a taxi and brought him home. Normally, they would have walked back after a cricket match.

Suresh still remembers the day clearly. When Uday had entered the house, complaining of pain from the ball hitting him on the head, Suresh had known instinctively that this did not bode well. He insisted on getting a surgeon to see his son. Being a Sunday, it was difficult to find a doctor, let alone a surgeon. He then contacted his Rotarian friend, Dr Gajendra Singh, who arrived in a taxi immediately. Even as

---

[33]Madhav Apte, an Indian cricketer was a Kanga League player. His cricket career spanned 55 years from 1948 to 2002.

Dr Gajendra spoke of the possibility of it happening, Uday slipped into a coma.

He was rushed to Jaslok Hospital in South Mumbai. The doctor had said to Suresh, 'You need to understand that your son has suffered from a brain haemorrhage. Had you come ten minutes late, we would not be able to save your son's life at all. Even now, we may be able to save your son, but we are not sure whether we will be able to save all his faculties.' The father could only nod and give his assent to the surgery.

This immediate action by the doctors saved Uday's life. But he was bed-ridden for months and lost a year at JBIMS. However, as Suresh says light-heartedly, 'People in our family say, "God knows what stimulus he got in his brain then. It made him a financial wizard".'

The family, especially his grandfather, Amritlal, were adamant. No more sports for Uday, especially cricket. Amritlal elicited a vow from Uday to never play cricket again in his life. He had a family business and excelled in studies. His career was not a question mark, Amritlal justified. Uday's one regret in life, even today, is that the intervention by fate cost him a career as a professional cricket player.

## COTTONED TO THE FAMILY BUSINESS

When Uday realized that his accident on the cricket field meant a year's loss in his educational pursuits, he decided that rather than lie around and mope about the sudden twist of fate, he would work in his family business. He persuaded the doctors to allow him to go to office.

At 20, Uday started attending office, located in Navsari Building in Fort area of Mumbai. There were 14 members of his family working in the same office building. As part of his work, he would go to Sewri, to the godowns. Uday speaks of this experience: 'I enjoyed what I did. What I learnt, which I consider the most important experience at the time, was the art of dealing with different kinds of people, including labour.' The experience also taught him about export processes like clearing and forwarding, shipping, etc.

Uday spent about nine months intricately involved with the working of the business, which gave him a perspective on operations. While he enjoyed what he was doing, he could see the family business in its true colours—as a system where age and hierarchy mattered more than merit—which disturbed him. He reflects,

> While you want to be part of the family business, how do you grow without a system of merit as a basis of evaluation? Also, who you are in the joint family dictates what is right. I realized that you may not necessarily have your way even if you are right. In those few months, I got into serious differences of opinion with others from the family.

These feelings stuck with him even as he returned to JBIMS to complete his MBA.

After the first year, as it was for most MBA students, it was time for a summer internship, which Uday completed at Hindustan Lever (now Hindustan Unilever Ltd). His internship report on reconciliation of Financial Accounting with Management Accounting was well appreciated by the company's Chairman, who offered a job to Uday after his second year. While Uday was sure he did not want to join the family business, he was in a dilemma whether or not to join a professional firm. So, he took the second year to make up his mind.

## DRAWN TO FINANCE

An important influence in his life during his MBA years was his professor of finance, Shivanand Mankekar. Uday still remembers Prof. Mankekar's first lecture. He recalls:

> He asked us, 'How do you value a company?'
> While someone said by net profit, another mentioned by assets, but Prof. Mankekar was not happy.
> He said, 'All wrong. You value a company on its cash flow.'

Mankekar was probably the Professor Higgins to Uday's Eliza Doolittle. He introduced Uday to the intricacies of the world of finance and explained to the fascinated young boy how companies grow. To take the learning experience further, Uday would accompany him to the stock market ,almost every day, to the office of a particular broker in the stock exchange building. He would sit there with the professor and observe the broker at work. Uday was fascinated to watch his guru deal in the stock market. It was probably around this time that the idea of a financial consultancy started to germinate in his mind and Uday began to read on the subject.

At the end of the second year at JBIMS, career decisions had to be made and father and son had a frank chat. Uday reminisces,

> My father asked me, 'Uday, what do you want to do in life?'

I said, I did not know. My interest is in finance and I want to work for some time as a professional and then look at the future. What I certainly shall not do is to join the family business. I don't want to have this problem of working with 14 family members and being one of the hands in the family business.

Uday wanted to script his own story and Suresh could understand this sentiment. He had noticed Uday's growing interest in finance over the past couple of years. Besides, he was aware of his family business and its deep family values and knew that Uday, with his brilliance, would be a misfit in the family business. Suresh acknowledged his son's acumen. He fondly recalled, 'Even while convalescing after his surgery, Uday was surpassing everyone in cotton trade, including myself. I knew he was slated for something different. I had to recognize his ability.'

At the same time, Suresh did not want Uday to get lost in the humdrum of a regular career, even if it were in an aspirational large corporate such as Hindustan Lever or Boston Consulting Group (BCG). Both were open to Uday. The latter had invited him to the US and offered him an opportunity to additionally pursue his studies. Both Amritlal and Suresh, dead set against Uday going to the US, almost 'quarrelled' with him. They were certain—in fact afraid—that Uday would excel if he went there, which would wipe out his aspiration of starting his own business or charting out an independent career as an entrepreneur. So, they made Uday an offer he could not refuse.

## AN ENTICING PROPOSAL

Suresh had a key role to play in the shaping of Uday as an entrepreneur. He offered Uday prime office space. He proposed, 'What if I convince the family and give you 300 sq ft of office space at Flora Fountain, opposite Handloom House, to work? What would you want to do then? Finance is your area. Start something there in finance.' Uday jumped at the offer and evinced his interest in setting up a financial consultancy.

Suresh went back to his family and put it up before the family council. The family agreed and Uday was given the office space to decide what he wanted to do. He was also sent to London for some practical training for three months under Phiroze Gutta, former Chairman of Central Bank of India and a friend of Suresh Kotak. Gutta had then joined BCCI in London as a senior director.

Following his return in 1982, Kotak & Co., the family firm, set up a separate division, Kotak Capital, with Uday in charge, in order to gain a foothold in the financial consulting space. When Uday had contemplated his first move, he had asked his father, 'Why don't you introduce me to your college friend, who is a big name in the financial market?' His father introduced him to Pradip Harkisandas of the stock broking firm Harkisandas Lakshmichand (HL), a large and well-reputed institutional brokerage firm, where H.T. Parekh of Housing Development Finance Corporation (HDFC) had begun his career. Pradip was one of the original four—the others being Bhupen Dalal, Hemendra Kothari and Nimesh

Kampani[34]—who were known as the big daddies of merchant banking in the 1970s and '80s. Pradip had even started HL Ficom Consultants, a merchant banking firm.[35]

Uday had explored the possibility of setting up a joint consulting venture for non-resident Indians (NRIs), 'NRI Consultancy', with Pradip. However, within six months of starting the NRI Consultancy venture with Pradip, in a partnership between HL and Kotak Capital, one of Pradip's family members over-speculated in the shares of Tata Steel and HL went bust on the stock exchange. Although Uday's venture was a separate one, he witnessed first-hand, the terrible shock of what could go wrong. With Pradip embroiled in the messy situation, their own joint venture (JV) was put on the back burner.

Around 1983 and '84, Uday met Sidney Pinto, the company secretary of the now erstwhile firm Imperial Chemical Industries (ICI), in Pradip's office. Pinto was one of the earliest merchant bankers of India, having set up the merchant banking division for Grindlays bank. He was also

---

[34]'Of Nimesh Kampani and the merchant bankers of the Yesteryears.' *BalaBlogs*, 3 August 2016, balablogsdotcom.wordpress.com/2016/08/03/of-nimesh-kampani-and-the-merchantbankers-of-the-yesteryears/. Accessed 4 July 2020.

[35]A merchant bank is a company that conducts underwriting, loan services, financial advising and fundraising services for large corporations and high net worth individuals. They are unlike commercial banks in that they do not offer services to the general public, such as checking accounts; nor do they collect deposits from the general public. These banks are experts in international trade, which makes them specialists in dealing with multinational corporations. Some of the largest merchant banks in the world include J.P. Morgan, Goldman Sachs, and Citigroup. ('Understanding Merchant Banks.' *Investopedia*, www.investopedia.com/terms/m/merchantbank.asp. Accessed 4 July 2020.)

involved with HL Ficom and was helping the family sort out its troubles. One day, when Uday was walking back with Pinto from the HL office at Nariman Point to his own office at Flora Fountain, Pinto asked him, 'Why don't you set up your own firm? Pradip has his own challenges to face.'

It must have been incredibly daunting for one so young to see the possible trials and tribulations that a career in finance could pose. There was always the safety of the family business to retreat into. Yet, by persevering with his original intent of establishing a financial consultancy, Uday demonstrated another important Shaper mindset, that of *Breaking Barriers.* It is this mindset which prompts shapers to navigate obstacles and act with strong determination.

Uday knew that his destiny was in finance and he refused to accept defeat even before he had started. Pinto's suggestion piqued his interest, and after some deliberation, he decided to work on setting up a separate company to undertake bill discounting and then leasing, both opportunities that emerged out of thin air.

## 'CHANCE' FORAYS INTO BUSINESS

Pinto introduced Uday to Farouk M. Irani, the founder of First Leasing Company of India in Chennai. It was one of only two leasing companies in India, as leasing itself was a new concept at the time. The other leasing company was $20^{th}$ Century Leasing Ltd. set up by Dev Ahuja. As First Leasing did not have a presence in Bombay, it found it difficult to compete in this city. In his meeting with Irani, Uday offered to be his lease broker, getting for him lease transactions in Bombay. Uday hired two junior staff members and started doing lease broking on behalf of First Leasing. He was now an entrepreneur in the world of finance.

Even the opportunity of a business in bill-discounting, that changed Uday's life, had similarly emerged out of the blue. Uday Phadke, one of Uday Kotak's friends from his MBA programme, had joined a Tata company called Nelco, where Ratan Tata had started his career. Nelco was in the business of radios and electronics and always found itself tight on working capital. As its suppliers had to be paid 90 days later, Nelco used to borrow money for 90 days at 17 per cent interest through bill discounting. Also, under the Credit Authorisation Scheme (CAS),[36] large companies like Nelco had a cap on the money they could raise from banks. The cap, at that time, was ₹5 crore. So, suppliers used to be in distress due to delay in payments.

Phadke made Uday a proposition. He said, 'If you have some affluent friends, Nelco will accept a bill of exchange. You arrange payment for the supplier. And at the end of 90 days, Nelco will pay back the money. It is a Tata company, after all.'

'At what rate of interest?' Uday asked.

'At 17 per cent' Phadke responded.

In those days, bank deposit rates (fixed deposit) were 6 per cent and lending rates were 17 per cent, as fixed by India's central bank. The differential was too good to be true. The banks were making a large spread and there was money to be made by anybody who could enter and find a way of reducing

---

[36]The Credit Authorisation Scheme (CAS) was launched by the government of India in 1965. Under this scheme, all commercial banks had to obtain prior RBI approval before granting a loan above a certain amount to a single borrower. As a control measure, it led to non-availability of adequate and timely credit and was abolished in 1989.

this spread. Uday could immediately see an opportunity area for his new business.

Uday then spoke with a few family and friends. He asked them, 'What is the interest rate you get on bank deposits?' With interest rates being part of a regulated regime, he would get a standard reply, 6 per cent. To which he would suggest, 'What if you got 12 per cent on a Tata risk?' The name Tata was synonymous with security.

They couldn't believe their ears. 'This boy is crazy. How can you get that?' they would ask incredulously. So long as the amounts were small, they were willing to take the risk. He raised small amounts from each contact ranging between ₹50,000 and ₹1 lakh.

Phadke was comfortable as long as Uday lent at the same rate as the banks. But Uday had other plans. He said to Phadke, 'You give me more business. I shall make the lending rate 16 per cent.'

Such bill-discounting was a serious business with narrow time margins. 'The money had to come into the account before the outgoing cheque was issued. The cheque would take 24-48 hours to clear, and within that time I would make sure that the refinancing would take place,' Uday states matter-of-factly. The fact however remains that Kotak got his first business with zero capital invested.

While there were other, more seasoned players in the financial sector at the time, Uday's ability to see the 'gap' set him apart as a Shaper. The 'leaders' would have had an equally strong knowledge of the technical environment that would be used to 'manage' the situation. However, a Shaper goes beyond merely knowing the environment. He is not only able to see the gaps, but also uses them to shape the environment in a manner that fits with the growing capabilities of the organization.

## STICKLER FOR RULES

Even while Uday seemed to have spotted a gap that others did not seem to have seen, he was plagued with doubt. As he puts it, 'The question was how do you do this business? You can't make this seem as a brokerage business.' More importantly, Uday's concern was whether the activity of bill discounting as they were doing it—buying and selling a bill—was legal. Was it within the framework of what the RBI allowed for a non-banking financial company (NBFC)? Uday did not wish to do anything remotely outside the purview of the law.

One of his college friends was Cyril Shroff, whose father Suresh Shroff owned and headed one of India's largest corporate law firms, Amarchand & Mangaldas & Suresh A Shroff & Co. (AMSS), founded in 1917. Uday would often spend his summer holidays with Cyril and his elder brother Shardul at their Lonavala home. Uday knew Suresh Shroff well. He therefore referred the bill discounting matter to Suresh for his counsel. AMSS examined this and cleared it saying it was based on the concept of the Bill Market Scheme, which the Narasimham Committee had actually strongly recommended back in 1970. However, Suresh Shroff was taking no chances. He advised, 'If you are going to start this business and make it bigger, you need to be sure.' He then got Justice P.N. Bhagwati, who had then retired as Supreme Court Chief Justice, to provide an opinion. Only after getting a go-ahead from his legal counsellors, did Uday throw himself into the bill discounting business.

We see in Uday's caution the Shaper mindset, which constantly evaluates the short-term, as well as the long-term. In the short-term, it was possible to make huge profits within the financial sector by playing with a gap. However, the big victory in the long-term could be achieved only when they survived to enjoy these profits.

Since that day, Uday has steadfastly held on to one institutional principle: 'Whatever you do, ensure that it is within the legal framework. Do not do anything outside the framework.'

And that is how Uday[37] got into doing bill discounting—the buying and selling of paper—while still a division of the family company. Uday explains the business,

> We bought at 16 per cent, and like a holder in due course, we endorsed it. I would give physical hundis[38] to investors, with invoices, challans, etc. As a bill of exchange is a negotiable instrument, we used to buy the bills, write the cheque, rediscount them and keep the spread. The banks were making 11 per cent; we were making 5 per cent. Due to the complexities of the interest rate system and the differential spread between the deposit and lending rates, where banks were working with the spread between 6 per cent and 17 per cent, we could intermediate and create a market. That is how we started and soon the business grew.

---

[37]Kotak Finance and other Kotak companies are referred to as Kotak in the narrative hereafter.
[38]A hundi is a financial instrument for use in trade and credit transactions.

## BRINGING IN THE BANKS

Kotak's business volumes grew, more so because bill discounting was not being done by the private sector in India at that stage. Kotak started buying and selling on a broader basis. His company approached banks too. However, banks had a problem due to the restrictions of the CAS, which imposed limits on the amount of credit they could extend to a single borrower. To overcome this issue, banks were willing to participate in the co-acceptance of bills, a concept that allowed sharing of the risk. Many of the foreign banks that had opened shop in India at the time, including banks like the European Asian Bank, Mitsui Bank, etc., did not have enough liquidity due to government regulations, which prevented them from having a deposit base in India. These banks were however, ready to take credit risk, then known as 'co-acceptance'. It helped that co-acceptance did not come under the limits imposed under the CAS.

On the other hand, older foreign banks like Standard Chartered, American Express, as well as some Indian banks, which had surplus cash, needed to find some use for it. So, Uday moved into arranging financing for the newer European banks. 'I didn't have to do much,' he recalls, 'it was all a question of getting a bill and then getting the bank to put its chhaapa (stamp) on it.' In such a case, it became an inter-bank risk. Thus, if a Nelco bill was co-accepted by a European Asian Bank, they could do an inter-bank risk transaction.

Uday details the working of this business,

I used to sit in my office opposite Handloom House. In the same area, we had multiple banks—two foreign banks and branches of some Indian banks too. As there were clear caps on the limit to which banks could lend to corporates, they would not book their exposure on their corporate account, but under inter-bank limits, which were more lenient. Mitsui and the other banks would take a charge from the drawee for a co-acceptance, and the interest would come to 16 per cent. We would take at 15 and rediscount at 13-14 per cent. So, there was a clean spread of 2-3 per cent and the risk was mitigated completely as these were banks which gave us scale. So, the whole business framework then was really built around business discounting, in addition to lease broking.

Kotak thus moved beyond individuals and bought bills and refinanced them from Indian banks. As Uday states, 'We made significant profits through the business of bill discounting because the market was imperfect and there was no concept of the private sector in financial services.'

He also speaks wistfully of the people who had believed in him at the time, especially V. Ananthakrishnan from Standard Chartered Bank, who later went on to become the Chief Executive of the Foreign Exchange Dealers Association of India (FEDAI). Uday says, 'Ananthakrishnan was a big supporter. He treated me like a protégé and Standard Chartered was one of our biggest re-discounters of Bills of Exchange followed by American Express and some nationalized banks as well.'

Kotak's success leads us to ask an obvious question: Why had no one else stumbled onto bill discounting? Uday responds with a shrug of his shoulders, 'Everyone was into leasing then, that was better known. People outside the banking sector did not know they could deal in negotiable instruments.'

## OF LOVE, MARRIAGE AND PARTNERSHIP

The year 1985 is a memorable one for Uday, when the three consecutive alphabets of the English language—KLM—had come together. It was the year he had started his own company, fallen in love with Pallavi, married her and also met Anand Mahindra who went on to play a key role in his life journey. We dwell on these three landmarks in Kotak's life, albeit not necessarily in that order.

In 1985, when they made a little money, Uday bought a broking card on the Bombay Stock Exchange (BSE) in his own name for about ₹2 lakh. Stock broking then could be done through a sole proprietorship or a partnership; not a company. As the bill discounting business grew in size, a formal business structure became necessary. On 21 November 1985, a separate company called Kotak Capital Management Finance Ltd. was formed, with Pinto playing an important role in the formation of this company. The company was backed by Uday, Pinto and Kotak & Co., the family business.

It was through his bill discounting business that he met Anand Mahindra in 1985. Uday reminisces, 'Anand had just returned from Harvard and joined Mahindra Ugine Steel as its General Manager (Commercial). Steel was always in need of working capital. I got to know Anand through one of the other Mahindra group companies' CFOs, who introduced us.'

When they met, Uday told Anand, 'We will raise money for you through bill discounting in 72 hours.' In those days, 72 hours was quick. That was the beginning of a relationship with Mahindra Ugine and Uday's own relationship with Anand Mahindra.

Uday met Pallavi, a graduate from Columbia University's

School of International and Public Affairs, at a friend's home. It was practically love at first sight! Pallavi had packed up her bags to go off to the US, where she wished to pursue a career. She changed her mind after meeting Uday. They were married within two months of dating.

At a pre-wedding function, Pinto told Anand, 'Uday is thinking of creating a separate company.' Anand said he would be happy to put money into a venture that Uday wanted to start and would participate in it. He didn't want control as he wasn't keen on the financial services business, but having returned from America, he knew the financial sector revolution would also hit India.

Kotak had studied the business models of some of the top financial services businesses in the West, like Goldman Sachs, JP Morgan, and other such firms. He admired these firms and believed that using the family name for one's company was a symbol of trust. He states,

> If you believe in yourself and the business, you should put your family name on the line. However, let's be honest. The Kotak name was not well-known then, but the addition of Mahindra's name gave the company instant credibility and recognition.

Uday thus asked Mahindra for a favour—to be able to associate the Mahindra name alongside his own in the new venture. Uday explained to Mahindra,

> We are in the business of reputation. Names matter. Let's put our names into the company. All the great financial houses—the Morgans, the Rothschild's and the others— are known by the names of their founders. Let's show

people that we care enough about this business to put our names on it.

Mahindra agreed to come on board, with a personal investment of ₹4 lakhs when the business took shape, apart from offering his family name. Uday needed ₹30 lakh to start his own NBFC. While he invested ₹13 lakhs and Kotak & Co. put in ₹5 lakhs, Uday raised the rest from family and friends. As Uday reminisces, 'I cast around desperately for investors and borrowed money to be able to buy my own stake. It took me nearly six months to raise the remaining eight-odd lakhs.' Anyone who wanted to put in money between November 1985 and April 1986 was brought on board. One of the founding investors was Kotak's father-in-law, based out of Surat, with his investment of ₹10,000! And thus, it was, that the name of Uday's company, Kotak Capital Finance Management Ltd. was changed to Kotak Mahindra Finance Ltd. (KMFL) in April 1986. With an initial equity capital of ₹30 lakhs, it started operating as an NBFC.

How can one capture the success of this fateful decision taken 35 years ago, by a young lad, all of 26, from a business family, who had decided to set his own trail? For those who would like to understand it in terms of statistics: If you had been one of Kotak's friends whom he had drawn upon for this original equity of ₹30 lakhs, and if you had invested ₹1 lakh at the time, your original investment would be worth over ₹2160 crores (at ₹1350/share) today!

The power of that compounding and the story of the transformation of an NBFC into one of India's most valuable banks follows in the next chapter.

# Chapter 4

# Strategic Nurturing

'Every problem is a gift—without problems
we would not grow.'

—Anthony Robbins, motivational speaker and writer

While KMFL was started as a JV with Mahindra, Uday also invited Anand's father, Harish Mahindra on board as Chairman, which he accepted. Two years later, the company was not only making money from bill discounting, but had also begun equipment leasing, which as Uday reminisces, was a 'popular tax shelter'. Uday also put to use the stock market card he had bought earlier. Around 1988, as the company was doing well, Harish advised him to move out of the small office space that his family had allowed him to use and move into a space more in keeping with his own aspirations. Uday realized it was time to shift gears and scale up. In keeping with the new organization he envisaged, Uday bought office space in Nariman Bhavan at Nariman Point. 'It was a big decision that, in hindsight, was crucial, as it helped us scale,' he admits.

## ENTERING CITI SPACE

Even while KMFL was riding a wave of success in the bill rediscounting space, another major opportunity presented itself to Uday in 1989, when Citibank entered the car financing business in India. This was the first time any bank had been allowed to finance cars in India, as the socialistic mindset prevalent earlier had frowned upon any form of consumerism. Citi offered customers car loans at a flat 13 per cent hire-purchase rate of interest, which remained the same even though the loan balance lowered, thereby taking the bank's internal rate of return to as much as 36 per cent. These car loans had become popular. Foreseeing opportunity, KMFL immediately entered the business of car financing. As an NBFC, it borrowed from banks to lend to customers against their vehicle as security. However, the major challenge was: How to compete with Citi, a premium foreign bank?

It is here that we witness signs of a Shaper mindset willing to *Break Barriers*. The barrier was Citibank's reputation and financial muscle as the big daddy of finance in those days. The solution lay in the environment within which the barrier had been created.

As Uday recalls,

We came up with an interesting solution. Maruti was [making] the most popular car then, with a six-month waiting period for delivery. So, we started the concept of booking cars in bulk, so that when the customer wanted, we could provide instant delivery. We would pre-book 5000 to 10,000 cars in our own name, effectively like a dealer would, but with the understanding that when the car was delivered, ownership would be moved to the customer's name. Thus, we were able to give our customers instant delivery. However, in those days, there was a high premium on the cars. We decided not to charge the premium, but customers who wanted the car from us on instant delivery terms had to get the car financed from us. The finance terms and interest rate were the same as Citibank—13 per cent. It worked and became a good business for us.

It was a fool-proof business model for which banks extended their credit line to KMFL against the cars being booked, which were then hypothecated to the banks. However, it was not smooth sailing. The size of Kotak's books was initially very small, just 50-100 cars, as its capacity to book was based on the funding it could get. So, it was essentially David taking on the mighty Goliath.

## LOCATION IS KEY

This is yet another instance, where his uniqueness becomes evident: Kotak was again able to spot an opportunity where no one else could. Anybody could have effectively adopted the same business model, or even the earlier one of bill-rediscounting, and could have gained from the opportunity of arbitrage. How was he able to succeed, where others could not even see the opportunity, let alone take advantage of it?

Uday reflects and answers somewhat modestly,

The location of my office was key to my early success because I would run with the bills of exchange myself. I would issue a cheque in the evening to a supplier in exchange for the bills. So, when I issued the cheques, I had the bills, but no money. Before the cheque hit the clearing, I had to ensure that the re-discounting happened and the money came into my account by morning. The supplier would put it in high value or first clearing and I could have been in big trouble if the cheque was dishonoured. So, I would go to the banks nearby to get these bills rediscounted and credit made into my company account. At Standard Chartered, I would wait outside Ananthakrishnan's room until he said, 'Come in.' He would then ask for the bills to be given to his operations. Or, I would run to American Express.[39] As time was of the essence, location was a big thing. Often, people do not understand the value of 'small things'.

There was skepticism about the business crucially resting on a time-based model. Of course, it required a deep understanding of the system as well as of how things worked. Uday agrees and then smilingly narrates a 'freak incident',

> As we grew, I had hired a peon. One day, when he was going from the Navsari Building office to American Express Bank at Flora Fountain—a distance of 500 m only, he accidentally dropped some bills of exchange. We had already issued the cheque. All of us then went hunting for the missing bills. Fortunately, we found the papers on a patch of grass and trees. How close to trouble can you be!

---

[39]Both Standard Chartered and American Express banks were located in the Fountain area, where Uday Kotak operated out of his family office space.

One can't help but wonder what kind of nerves it would have required for someone barely 30 to be doing this. For Kotak Mahindra Finance, 1989 was the turning point and by the early 1990s the company had become the largest bill discounting firm in the country, aggressively gaining market share. Uday and KMFL were unstoppable.

## INTEREST IN CAPITAL MARKETS

It was time to look at other means of growth. Uday had a stock broking card in his name, but he wasn't active in stock broking. This changed shortly after Uday was invited to the high-profile wedding of Ambani scion, Anil Ambani, with Tina Munim, a Bollywood actor, in February 1991. Among the invitees was Rikeen Dalal, son of Pradip, Uday's first partner who had died in an air crash in 1988. Although Uday's NRI Consulting venture with Pradip had not taken off, life had come full circle. As Uday and Dalal exchanged pleasantries, Dalal informed him that he was focused on strengthening Ficom Organics—a chemicals company—and was planning to close down HL Ficom, the merchant banking firm that his father had started. Considering that the firm had a broking, distribution, investment banking and deposit gathering business, Uday asked Dalal, 'If you are closing it down, why don't you give it to me?' Dalal considered the offer and agreed. Thus, in April 1991, Kotak bought the office space and franchise for HL Ficom and activated the business of stock-broking and deposit distribution in his sole proprietary firm. A few months later, Kotak went public in December 1991 and KMFL came to be better known and recognized.

## INVESTING IN BANK OF MADURA

In February 1992, with destiny inexorably leading him towards banking, Uday received a call from Dr Karumuttu Thiagarajan Chettiar, the Founder of Loyal Textile Mills Ltd. and a doyen of the textile industry in South India. Uday's family had professional connections with Dr Thiagarajan and Suresh knew him well. Dr Thiagarajan had a 20 per cent stake in the Bank of Madura, a private sector bank founded by his father in Madurai in 1943 and wanted Uday to come on board as a shareholder and become active in the banking sector.

In order to understand Dr Thiagarajan's motivation for approaching Kotak, we need to look at the economic climate pertaining to banking in India and the shareholding pattern of private banks at the time. While there existed 'old' private sector banks, relics from pre-Independence times, which had been allowed to continue even after nationalization, prevailing banking regulations in 1992 had closed banking to the private sector. Thus, new entrepreneurs or even large NBFCs desirous of entering banking had no choice but to buy into the banking business. For instance, an interesting advertisement with a deceptively simple caption was carried in a Madras[40] news daily on 14 April 1992. It read: 'Wanted: To take over a bank. A well established and fast-growing industrial group having the best potential for diversification is keenly interested to take over a banking company.' It was an era when more and more private banks, except of course the unprofitable ones, were becoming targets of aggressive

---

[40]Chennai, the capital of the Indian state of Tamil Nadu, was then known as Madras.

take-overs. One way of staving off such takeover bids was to enter into strategic alliances of the type that Bank of Madura sought with Kotak Mahindra Finance.

The Bank of Madura was controlled by the Chettiar community—the indigenous banking community of the South—to which Thiagarajan belonged. The Chairman, S.B. Sabapathy and his family held a mere 5 per cent, while the rest of the shares were held among many large and small shareholders. Only Dr Thiagarajan singularly held the largest chunk of 20 per cent.

Thiagarajan offered Uday 50 per cent of his own stake. Uday was interested. His vision was to establish KMFL as a broad-based financial services company, which included banking. The deal offered Uday an opportunity to get into something he would have found difficult to enter into from scratch. Going forward, he expected the treasury sector and the non-fund areas to turn out most profitable. Sabapathy had stated at the time, 'This strategic alliance was the best defence to fight take-over bids.'[41]

However, some legalities needed to be ironed out. As per the RBI rules at the time, a company could not own more than 1 per cent share in any one entity. Uday had to ensure that KMFL had 10 separate legal entities, each with a different name, so that the 10 per cent stake could be bought in the name of its 10 different entities. Thus, KMFL and its associates acquired a stake in the Bank of Madura on 9 April 1992. As key stakeholders, the company got a board seat at the bank.

---

[41]'Strategic Alliance of Banks Emerges As Best Defence to Fight Take-over Bids.' *India Today*, 2 Sept. 2013, www.indiatoday.in/magazine/economy/story/19920515-strategic-alliance-of-banks-emerges-as-best-defence-to-fight-take-over-bids-766257-2013-08-17. Accessed 4 July 2020.

Four nominees of Kotak Mahindra Finance, including Uday and Suresh Shroff, joined the Bank of Madura Board in a non-executive position, which caught the headlines in a major way then.

Uday remembers the drama surrounding the purchase of the stake. Before they bought the stake, Uday called upon S. Venkitaramanan—the RBI Governor at the time and told him they were planning to buy a stake in the Bank of Madura. Venkitaramanan cautioned them about the bank being a Chettiar bank and Thiagarajan himself being a Chettiar. He also asked Uday, 'Does A.C. Muthiah know?' A.C. Muthiah, a leading Chettiar industrialist and owner of Southern Petrochemicals Industries Ltd. (SPIC), owned about 5 per cent stake in the Bank of Madura.[42] Uday frankly assumed that Thiagarajan would have told him. He only knew that he was buying through 10 separate entities, in keeping with the law. Only after Venkitaramanan gave them the nod, was the deed done and the deal signed.

It was around the same time, that the government of India was considering opening up the banking sector. When Kotak acquired a stake in the Bank of Madura, their own stock of KMFL was listed. As per existing regulations, the shares issued in December took three months to get listed. The stock had been issued at ₹45 per share but was listed at ₹1300 per share in April 1992. However, as Uday puts it candidly, 'These

---

[42]A.C. Muthiah was later accused of insider trading in the run-up to the Bank of Madura merger with ICICI Bank, announced in December 2000. 'SEBI Report On BoM Finds Muthiah Negotiated Deal With B Arun Kumar.' *The Financial Express*, 23 March 2002, www.financialexpress.com/archive/sebi-report-on-bom-finds-muthiah-negotiated-deal-with-b-arun-kumar/41042/. Accessed 4 July 2020.

prices had more to do with what was happening in the stock market at that time, than what we had done.' The 'Big Bull' Harshad Mehta had been gaming the markets then, leading to the collapse of the entire securities system. A vexing time was brewing.

While the Bank of Madura deal did not undulate as smoothly as Kotak had expected, even its stock market foray was not completely uncontroversial. It was the beginning of several storms that Uday had to face in his incredible journey as a banker.

## SECURITIES SCAM SHOCKS BUSINESS

The first storm erupted on 23 April 1992, when Sucheta Dalal, a journalist, exposed a securities scam on the front page of the national news daily, *The Times of India*.[43] Euphemistically called the Bombay Securities Scam of 1992, it was possibly the biggest financial scam in Indian history until then. The Janakiraman Committee, the Joint Parliamentary Committee set up by the RBI to investigate the scam, put the losses at ₹4300 crores, which, if adjusted for inflation, would amount to more than ₹24000 crores today.[44] There were political ramifications as well, with the key accused Bombay-based broker Harshad Mehta implicating then Prime Minister, P.V. Narasimha Rao in the scandal, alleging that in November 1992 he had paid ₹1 crore to the PM for political patronage.

---

[43]She herself is said to have got the tip-off after she saw him pulling up at the State Bank of India offices in a brand-new Toyota Lexus, which had just been released internationally and which cost more than Rs. 40 lakhs at the time.
[44]To put this in perspective, the latest Nirav Modi-Punjab National Bank Scam estimated losses of Rs. 13000 crores.

The consequences of the scam impinged on Uday and Kotak Mahindra Finance.

The securities scam[45] of 1991-92 was a systematic fraud involving the Indian banking sector and the stock markets, which had been 'gamed' by a set of stockbrokers, led by Mehta, as the kingpin. This band of stockbrokers had exploited the loopholes in the system to siphon off funds from interbank transactions. Bank funds worth ₹3500 crores were diverted to these stockbrokers, who then channelled these funds to buy large volumes of stocks across sectors, resulting in huge rises in the Sensex. The market Sensex rose from 1194 to over 4500 points, with stocks like ACC surging from about ₹200 per share to about ₹9000 per share during this period.

The scam was rooted in the deep knowledge that brokers like Harshad Mehta and his associates possessed regarding the banking system, especially the inter-bank transactions that happened between banks with 'surplus' and 'deficit' funds. Opportunities for fraud arose with such transactions being undertaken through brokers like Mehta since only the broker knew both the parties involved.

The chief irregularities were in the misuse of Bankers' Receipts (BRs), which were supposed to be traded only between banks in lieu of government securities. Brokers, in collusion with some banks, however, began to use BRs in lieu of securities traded. Thus, in reality, only BRs changed hands, not the securities.

With markets experiencing tremendous surge, the

---

[45]'The Harshad Mehta case: Where time has overtaken justice by a mile.' *The Economic Times*, 5 July 2016, https://economictimes.indiatimes.com/news/politics-and-nation/the-harshad-mehta-case-where-time-has-overtaken-justice-by-a-mile/articleshow/53052771.cms. Accessed 4 July 2020.

underlying securities themselves were sold at profits, and the BR would be retired when it was time to return money to the banks. Mehta struck such deals across banks and rolled the money at every pay-out-level.

The investigation agencies arrested Mehta in November 1992. He was charged with over 70 criminal cases, mostly relating to bribery, cheating, forgery, criminal conspiracy and falsification of accounts and over 600 civil action suits.

Even as India was opening up its markets to the world in 1991, and even as Harshad Mehta was planning and carrying out the audacious scam which would go down as one of the first and worst financial scams of India, Uday was taking baby steps towards going international. He could not, however, be left untouched by the impact of the securities scam on India's financial world.

## TIE-UP WITH GOLDMAN SACHS

In 1990-91, when India adopted Privatization, Liberalization and Globalization, and Manmohan Singh became India's Finance Minister, the capital markets opened up and trading in Global Depository Receipts (GDRs)[46] was initiated. In March 1992, about nine months after Singh's dream budget, Euromoney[47] held its first international conference in Delhi.

---

[46]Global Depository Receipts are securities certificates issued by intermediaries such as banks in more than one country for facilitating investments in foreign companies. A GDR represents a certain number of shares in a foreign company that is not traded on the local stock exchange. The shares in the GDR trade on their domestic stock exchange.

[47]Euromoney Conferences is the world's leading organizer of events for capital markets and investment professionals that works to connect companies and

Euromoney Conferences sought to inform and explain the latest trends in global financial markets, besides acting as impartial forums for the rigorous exchange of ideas. These conferences provided a platform where people could make new connections and forge profitable business relationships.

Kotak wished to attend this conference just for an opportunity to connect with Goldman Sachs because, as he understood it, it was *the* firm to go to for a tie up—being 'blue-blooded and all that', as he puts it. Uday hence checked out the guest list of the 1992 Euromoney Conference. Among the invitees, there was Tingu Khatau, from the Khatau family in Mumbai representing the London Goldman office. Among the three members from Goldman on the guest list, there was an Indian named Vinod Ahuja, who had become a partner in Goldman because of his expertise in operations and technology. Uday wanted to connect with Ahuja through this conference and see where the relationship could go.

Uday met Ahuja and his associates from Goldman Sachs in March 1992 and discussed with them possible collaborations. They invited him to New York for further discussions and in May 1992, Uday was in New York. At the time, Goldman had no presence in Asia, except in Japan. India had held relatively low interest for Goldman, until they met Uday. It marked the beginning of Kotak's agency relationship with Goldman Sachs.

Uday offered to market Goldman in India and to connect them with the companies they were interested in and approved of. Out of the GDR fees they made, Uday asked for a 25 per cent share. So, if Goldman charged 3 per cent GDR

---

governments with the financial institutions that support their growth.

fee, as their Indian agent, Kotak would get 25 per cent of that.

Kotak was much smaller than Goldman at the time. What made Goldman enter this relationship? Goldman of course carried out its due diligence in working with KMFL as their agent. However, here again, we witness the characteristic that is typical of Shapers, which is that of building enduring relationships constituting social capital, which can be actually relied upon during times of need.

The Goldman relationship, as Uday attests, was in equal measure due to the fortuitous presence of one of his earlier acquaintances at Goldman—Sanjiv Misra, who had been with the Mumbai branch of the Bank of America earlier. Two to three years prior to approaching Goldman, Uday used to deal with Sanjiv in the Bank of America office for bill rediscounting. Sanjiv had later moved to Goldman and that relationship had also helped him.

Kotak's relationship with Goldman was that of a pure agency; it was not a JV at this stage. Kotak would help get GDR mandates of companies such as Arvind Mills. The client selection was entirely up to Goldman. If Goldman approved of the client, they would handle it and give Kotak 25 per cent of the GDR fee; Kotak would handhold the client and do everything else.

## TROUBLESOME TIMES

While Uday was in New York, discussing an agency relationship with Goldman Sachs, the security scam had already broken out and brought along unexpected damage. Front page newspaper headlines loudly proclaimed Bank of Madura's involvement in the scam. S.B. Sabapathy was the

Chairman of the Bank of Madura at that time. Fortunately, as Kotak had recently come on board and owned about 9.9 per cent of the shares with RBI acknowledgement, it did not get its fingers heavily burnt even though for Uday, the stench around this news was unacceptable, given that banking itself was a business based on trust.

This was a period of introspection and learning for our Shaper. As Uday reflects,

> After we got into the Bank, we realized that there was an ongoing battle among the Chettiars and Muthiah and Dr Thiagarajan for control of the Bank. The whole thing blew up on 29 May 1992 when I was in New York. There were stories in the papers that Uday Kotak had buzzed off to the US because he didn't want to face these issues. We were not even in control of the Bank. We had just appointed a couple of people on the board. It became a big issue. So, we then said, let's lie low. Let's not focus on Bank of Madura. Let's focus on our company. The biggest learning for me happened during 1992-94.

The situation worsened in July 1992, when some of the large corporates were again found to be using bill discounting for accommodation financing. The RBI banned bill rediscounting and overnight Kotak found that 60 per cent of its revenue source had been wiped out.

Fortunately, KMFL had already started equipment leasing on its own balance sheet, an activity carried out essentially for tax shelter purposes. It was also in the capital market. 'Thank God, we had entered the capital markets business,' says Uday,

The Indian stock market was like a well back then, inward looking. We knew however, that the capital markets would develop. As we didn't know much about the business, we set up an agency for Goldman Sachs. A basic partnership as an agent to match global investors with Indian issuers of American Depository and Global Depository Receipts which started in 1992, transformed into a JV for investment banking and stock broking in 1995.

Fortunately, the relationships that Kotak had so meticulously and painstakingly forged started to yield results at a time when some doors were being shut.

## NEW WINDOWS OPEN FOR BUSINESS

How did Uday get Goldman to enter into a JV—its very first anywhere in the world? Uday narrates the 'little story', which goes back to 1993,

A Canadian, Mark Evans, who was an Olympic gold medallist in rowing, with his twin brother, Mike, who is now Vice Chairman of Alibaba, was incharge of Goldman Asia, headquartered in Hong Kong. I had good relations with Mark. One day, Mark called me and said, 'Uday, I have a couple of senior partners from the US coming in. Fly down and meet them over dinner in Hong Kong.' So, I just took the plane and met them over dinner. I had also requested Anand to accompany me for this meeting. The two partners from US were Jon Corzine and

Hank Paulson.[48] They were becoming more interested in India and wanted to know about opportunities in this country. At the end of the meeting, after dinner, they spoke to Mark and asked, 'Can we hire this guy?' So Mark said, 'No. He wants to build a business.' I said, 'I would be delighted to partner with Goldman. But I want my own space.'

Sometime after that meeting, in 1994, we got Hank to come to India—his first visit with his wife. I requested Anand and Harish to host them in Coorg, where Anand had a holiday home, as Hank was fond of birding. So, they had a small holiday and that's how the relationship with Hank blossomed. In July 1995, we entered into a JV with Goldman to do investment banking and broking. The alliance was mainly driven by Hank. He was still not the chairman but was moving up the ranks. It happened to be Goldman's first JV anywhere in the world and ran for 10 years.

The JV with Goldman Sachs for investment banking was called Kotak Mahindra Capital Company (KMCC), created as a subsidiary of KMFL. Another company, Kotak Securities was also set up as a JV with Goldman Sachs to carry out the broking business.

Another critical JV with Ford Credit was also initiated around this time. In 1996, Mahindra & Mahindra had entered into a JV with Ford Motor Co. Ford Motor wanted Ford Credit to have a presence in India. So, Anand referred them to Uday, who formed a JV in the car finance business with Ford Credit

---

[48]Incidentally, both Corzine and Paulson became chairmen of Goldman Sachs at different points of time later.

International, called Kotak Mahindra Primus Ltd., also a subsidiary of KMFL. These two JVs—one with Goldman Sachs and the other with Ford Credit—helped KMFL build its capital and fortify its presence.

Kotak started to grow in other areas as well. In 1998, Kotak entered the mutual fund market with the launch of Kotak Mahindra Asset Management Company. In 2000, when the insurance business opened up in India, Kotak Mahindra went into life insurance through a tie-up with South Africa's Old Mutual plc. All these were set up as subsidiaries of KMFL.

## SHIFTING GEARS

While these new businesses were opportunities for expansion, Uday's heart was set on the banking business and soon enough, an opportunity opened up. On 2 January 2001, Dr Bimal Jalan, then RBI Governor announced the opening up of the Indian banking sector to private sector banks by giving out new bank licenses and released the guidelines for new private sector banks.

During the three months provided to file the application for a banking license, there was intense discussion amongst the KMFL team: 'To be or not to be.' The team quickly concluded that in the short run, for the first five to six years, they would probably lose a lot of money, but it was a business which would take off after that.

Backed by this belief, Kotak applied for a banking licence, clear in his mind about its importance, especially after the stock market crisis. On the one hand, was his aspiration to be a major financial player led by a bank. On the other, were the deep learnings from the aftermath of the NBFC crisis in 1997-

98, which had led to 85-90 per cent of NBFCs succumbing to the crisis.

While KMFL had survived the crisis, Uday realized that there were inherent challenges and weaknesses in an NBFC business model. Then, there was a third driver, which was the strong capital base that the NBFC had built as a result of the huge amounts of capital received through the deals with the two foreign JV partners—Goldman Sachs and Ford Credit—in 1995-96. 'The capital structure infusion of the Ford Credit JV was in the form of a hockey stick, with capital flowing in continuously from 1996 to 2003,' says Uday.

KMFL was a profitable company by all standards when it received an in-principle approval from RBI in 2002, which was valid for a year, to enable applicants to mobilize the ₹200 crore (₹2 billion) start-up capital and fulfil other conditions, based on the recommendations of a high-level committee chaired by former RBI Governor, I.G. Patel.

Even as Uday was debating the bank structure as a separate company, the RBI directives were released, which required that the parent company be converted into a bank. Banking, as he could see it, was going to be a major money guzzler. 'We asked ourselves, "Where would the money for banking come from? More important, why transition from the highly profitable NBFC to banking? Did it really add up?"' Uday recalls the deliberations.

The math was all wrong. In the first five to six years, banking would be a losing business compared to the NBFC. It did not even look like a business which had a similar net value accretion as an NBFC when you kept getting your funds. 'It was an extremely difficult phase and we were lucky,' Uday admits.

Finally, when Kotak took the call, it was a leap of faith. 'We felt that if we have to be a sound, stable, strong financial institution in India serving customers, we must have the banking platform. It was a conviction call,' Uday states. In February 2003, Kotak received permission from the RBI to convert the NBFC into a bank. The rest, as they say, is history.

How did Uday manage to shift gears ever so often, going through extreme situations—his Agni Pariksha or 'Trial by Fire' as he calls it—as he went about creating the organization of his dreams within an environment that can, at the very least, be called 'unfriendly'? While the transformation of an NBFC into a Scheduled Commercial Bank was accomplished within two decades, its metamorphosis into an institution was achieved within the next two decades as we shall see in the next chapter.

Chapter 5

# Building a Bank

You can't build a great building on a weak
foundation. You must have a solid foundation if
you're going to have a strong superstructure.

—Gordon B. Hinckley, American Clergyman

K otak Mahindra Bank (KMB) a new private sector bank
was born in February 2003. The decision to transform
itself from an NBFC to a commercial bank was the result of
long deliberations among the core Kotak Mahindra team.
Its consultants, McKinsey & Co. had advised KMFL on the
business strategy, while the Delhi-based company Momentum
and an individual called Vivek Kamath (ex-Trikaya Grey) had
advised them on creating the bank's brand. A Bangalore based
firm Ray & Keshavan made the logo. Software firm iFlex
worked on the bank's technology platform.

## EXITING BANK OF MADURA

The seeds of this transformation, however, were sown more
than a decade ago, when Dr Thiagarajan persuaded Kotak to
buy a stake into Bank of Madura in 1992. This move was, as
we have seen, mis-timed. While Kotak had decided to lie low

in the aftermath of the Harshad Mehta scam in April 1992, Dr Thiagarajan himself took charge as Executive Chairman and turned around the bank. By 1998-99 however, as Dr Thiagarajan's health began to fail, he wanted Uday—the holder of 10 per cent equity stake in his bank—to acquire Bank of Madura or merge it with KMFL. Uday, though bitten by the banking bug, decided not to increase his stake in the bank.

Uday understood the sensitivities and challenges. He reasoned that it was a Chettiar Bank with strong community linkages under the jurisdiction of Tamil Nadu state, and moreover, if they merged, the new entity would need to carry the name of Bank of Madura as KMFL was still an NBFC. The name was an emotive issue for Uday who discussed the matter with his team and concluded that it made no sense to merge Bank of Madura. Acquiring it and keeping it as an independent entity also made no sense, as this would pose issues regarding brand dilution. Kotak thus sold its shareholding in Bank of Madura—acquired by ICICI Bank[49] in February, 2001—and thus exited this business.

Yet the ambition and aspiration to be a large financial services company with a banking business still remained—an aspiration that predated the entry of other banks like HDFC, ICICI, UTI bank and others, which appeared on the banking scene only in 1994, not as commercial banks, but as development financial institutions.[50] Prior to 1994, there was

---

[49]'ICICI Bank, Bank of Madura boards approve merger.' *Times of India*, 12 December 2000, https://timesofindia.indiatimes.com/ICICI-Bank-Bank-of-Madura-boards-approve-merger/articleshow/11443736.cms. Accessed 4 July 2020.
[50]Development financial institutions were set up to provide development/project finance which was essentially long-term in nature, as opposed to

no way one could acquire a license to start one's own bank.[51]

'We closed one chapter and moved onto another when we applied for a banking license in 2001. The linkage is important, since the aspiration to get into banking had been there from 1991 when we took the 10 per cent stake in Bank of Madura,' clarifies Uday.

## A CAPITAL DECISION

Setting up a new bank needed funds. Luckily for Kotak, the capital markets were surging at the time, with Indian equity markets entering a period of a bull run between April 2003 and January 2008, which remains unrivalled till date. Lasting 246 weeks, the equity markets experienced a 614 per cent increase over this period. Led by high infrastructure sector investment and global liquidity being available, the BSE Sensex went from 2924 points on 25 April 2003 to 20873 on 8 January 2008.[52]

---

commercial banks which used short-term deposits for giving out short-term loans. These were largely majority-owned by the government and catered to the long-term development needs such as infrastructural needs.

[51]The only exception was the first new generation private sector bank, IndusInd Bank, promoted by the non-resident Indian businessman, Srichand P. Hinduja. The bank received its license in 1994, more due to a 'good marketing strategy' when it appealed to the government with the claim that while it had not recognised the Sindhi community through granting it a separate state in the aftermath of the Partition of India in 1947, it could do so by at least allowing a bank for the Sindhi community. This strategy worked and IndusInd bank was incorporated in 1994.

[52]Bhaskar, Anoop. 'What the Past 6 Bull Runs Tell Us About This Market.' *Mint*, 27 Oct. 2014, www.livemint.com/Money/XMTtBng0BtRHpU6PCocUrL/Will-the-current-market-uptrend-last-for-long.html; 'Will Top Performers of Last Five Bull Runs Roar This Time Around?' *The Economic Times*, 29 Mar. 2019, economictimes.indiatimes.com/markets/stocks/news/will-top-performers-of-last-five-bull-runs-roar-this-time-around/articleshow/68627457.cms. Accessed 4 July 2020.

Many businesses rode this boom in the global capital markets. KMB in India was one of them.

Its capital-market-based businesses were working well and KMCC was by then India's leading investment bank while Kotak Securities was India's largest broking firm. Together, they contributed to profits after tax of ₹523 crores in FY 2008, when the total group profit (consolidated after tax) was ₹991 crores.[53] Such a healthy performance by Kotak Mahindra Bank's key subsidiaries, KMCC and Kotak Securities Ltd., helped in sustaining market confidence on consolidated profits as the basis for the stock price of the firm.

Uday admits that were it not for this capital market boom, they would have faced a nagging debt problem. He also admits that they were consistently making expenditures and investments towards their foray into banking for the first five to six years, spending on infrastructure, restructuring, technology and people, and were losing money every year. The boom in the global capital markets during this crucial period, he reiterates, helped them endure the problem of debt and availability of capital. One of the first moves was to man the new organization.

## SETTING UP THE TEAM

A strong team was needed to pull off the banking business. Uday had people in his core team who were finance professionals, but had no experience of banking. So, the

---

[53]'Kotak Mahindra Bank Ltd Earnings Update FY2002-2003.' *Kotak Mahindra*, 23 June 2003, http://www.kotak.com/bank/pressroom/pdf/KotakMahindraBankFY03EarningRelease.pdf. Accessed 4 July 2020.

question was, 'How to proceed into a new venture?' For a while, Uday contemplated bringing in an external CEO to run this new business, and recalled even interviewing a few people, but he soon dropped the idea and went about putting together his own crew.

Uday remembers,

> We decided that the core team for the bank project would be the same team of eight—the finance and non-banker guys, who would carry the project forward and deliver. Additionally, we would get about three external people, essentially bankers, to become a part of the core team.

The core team for the project comprised professionals who had spent long years in the different KMFL subsidiaries and had built the company—Kotak's senior management team. These included Dipak Gupta, Shanti Ekambaram, Shivaji Dam, Gaurang Shah, K.V.S. Manian, Narayan S.A., Jaimin Bhatt and C. Jayaram in addition to Uday himself. The 'outsiders' recruited in 2002 after getting the in-principle approval of the RBI—Mohan Shenoi, Arvind Kathpalia and Ajay Sondhi—were all bankers, with several years of experience working in top banks including ICICI, Standard Chartered and Citibank/UBS. They were recruited to head sensitive core banking functions including Treasury, Operations, Risk and Technology and Corporate and Investment Banking.

It was an unconventional decision to start the business of banking with a core group of inexperienced non-bankers and expect them to make it a success. But Uday knew his people. In Uday's words, they were people with passion and purpose, with middle-class values. They had great confidence and trust in each other and worked well as a team. He was confident that this team could pull it off with the expertise of the external trio who were bankers by profession.

As the larger part of the core group was inexperienced, the next decision was human resource allocation—who would do what. Each of the team members was put in charge of an activity they had never done before, yet went on to excel in it. Together, they went on to create a successful bank known for its family-like culture, together with high passion and professionalism. 'We spent one year between 2002 to 2003, planning and working on our transition from a small NBFC to a little bank,' says Uday with a touch of humility.

It was indeed a period of humungous learning for the core team. Shanti Ekambaram, who joined KMFL in 1991 to run its trade finance business, had risen through the ranks to become the Executive Director and CEO, KMCC. She remembers the initial few months of setting up the bank as the best time in her life because for the first time she did not 'have to chase revenue targets'. Setting up a bank, however, needed people, and her 'only' target was to hire a few hundred people every week and ensure timelines for the set-up. Her first role in KMB was to set up its wholesale banking business. Uday had announced that the bank would begin its operations before the end of fiscal 2003. Shanti undertook the work of drafting the credit, trade and other policies and operational procedures for the bank, which as a non-banker, she had no clue about. She laughs and remembers how she had written these policies by looking at the policies of other banks.

## BUILDING PROCESSES AND BRANCHES

Moving from being an NBFC to a bank required shedding the earlier skin and taking on a new one. Banking being a highly regulated business necessitated that. The bank as a platform provided exposure to compliance, regulation, processes and controls, different from the way in which Kotak had operated previously.

Shanti recollects,

> In the first five years, I found this extremely difficult, as we were used to taking instant decisions and moving on. In the earlier ecosystem, if I found something I was struggling with, I didn't have to write a long note and get a sign off from eight different people. I just went ahead and executed it. But that was no longer possible; we had to have processes. We realized that we couldn't scale without putting processes into place.

There were core team members who specialized in setting up systems and processes to mitigate risks. Apart from the entrepreneurial Shanti, Dipak, with his long stint at Ford Credit JV, had process etched into his DNA and helped in the transformation of the NBFC into a deeply process-oriented bank.

Once Kotak had its people and the funds, it had to build trust, the most important ingredient in banking—which meant more than just a posh address at Nariman Point.

A simple incident, right at the beginning of his banking journey, drove home this lesson for Uday. He narrates,

> We had received the banking license from RBI and were all set to inaugurate our first branch at Mittal Court in

Nariman Point on 22 March 2003. A grand function was organized with the RBI Governor and other important guests in attendance. One of our marketing guys who stayed with his father in Vashi went home after the launch and told his father, 'Papa, a new bank is open. It is a very good bank.' The old man replied, 'You say a bank has opened, but where is the bank?' He came back and told me this story. It was an important lesson for me. For a bank to build the trust and confidence among its depositors, it has to be seen and heard and felt.

Building such trust required a rapid expansion of the bank's branches. While the RBI had given Kotak permission to convert 30 KMFL branches spread across 20 locations into bank branches, the problem was that most of these branches were located on higher floors of buildings in remote parts of cities across the country; hardly the kind of place where people would go and undertake their banking business. So, these branches had to be relocated and converted into ground floor branches. One of the early tasks that KMB had was to set up and then expand the number of branches. By 2003-04, it had managed to open 30-32 branches, within just 14 months. As the organization evolved, KMB built trust through its smooth processes and protocols, even as it spread its branches and carved out its reputation as a valuable bank.

## OF SELF BELIEF AND CHUTZPAH

How did a small bank evolve into a valuable bank? Within six months of KMB becoming a bank, Maruti Suzuki came out with an Initial Public Offering (IPO). KMB wanted to become the bankers for the issue, as it would be a prestigious assignment to start with. Shanti shared a good rapport with Maruti, as she had dealt with this company in her previous role. However, the manager responsible for the IPO at Maruti told Shanti quite frankly, 'You have one and a half branches. How will you manage an IPO this large?' The barb, though sharp, had an element of truth. It was true that KMB had one branch in Mumbai and had just started a branch in Delhi. Yet, Shanti persisted and insisted that KMB was the right choice to handle the IPO. Maruti agreed to take on KMB as their banker.

A six-member team was set up in KMB that worked day and night to learn everything they needed to know. Finally, as Shanti asserts,

> We worked hard and collected 60 per cent of the issue proceeds across 60 locations with our 'one and a half branches'. Nobody expected us to pull it off. But it was only about two things: One, we knew our capital markets; Two, we wanted to prove ourselves.

This bold and enthusiastic attitude to business infused with dollops of self-belief and chutzpah brought in a huge amount of money in the very first year of KMB's existence as a bank.

## A CULTURE OF CONSERVATISM

Building the bank's culture, especially that pertaining to risk, was based on KMB's own learnings in its earlier avatar as an NBFC and the survival techniques picked up along the way. KMFL experiences of Asset-Liability Management

(ALM) Risk,[54] especially during the 1999 NBFC crisis, or of how badly lending could wreck the organization, shaped the institution's credit and risk culture and imbued its processes with conservatism.

Kotak built itself as a cautious corporate bank. Conservative in its lending, it went into IPOs, cash management and trade finance, in which it had the expertise; but avoided infrastructure financing. The policy in KMB spelt 'careful' when it came to lending to companies and how much to lend to each. Dipak had a comment, which others love to quote, 'I can stand on Marine Drive and barter money, but getting it back is more important.'

KMB avoided large exposures and its attitude to risk was measured. This culture of conservatism and low exposure also came from an understanding of its net worth, which was still small. The hands-on experience with risk also resulted in KMB not putting all its eggs into one basket, which is reflected in the growth of its subsidiary companies to 18, over the years.[55] Uday explains succinctly, 'In the banking business, errors of commission are more expensive than errors of omission. In the investing business, it is the other way round. Errors of omission are more expensive than errors of commission.'

Here then, was a company which understood itself and its right place under the sun. The future beckoned, and yet it knew that one had to take each step cautiously, carefully considering all the learnings of the past. It also knew from

---

[54]The latter referred to the risk a bank ran when it had a mismatch between its assets (essentially loans) and liabilities (essentially deposits).
[55]For the full list of subsidiaries, see https://www.kotak.com/en/investor-relations/governance/subsidiaries.html.

the mistakes of its peers in its earlier life as an NBFC, that the worst mistakes are often made at the best of times. This learning was as applicable in its new banking identity as it was for its NBFC avatar. Although conservative, KMB was a company which could adapt quickly by shedding its old skin and donning a new one.

## WE ARE BUSINESS PEOPLE

Even as the bank started building scale and adopting processes, entering new businesses meant risk, which it managed to reconcile with its own preference for conservatism, by staying focused on risk-adjusted returns. To do this, KMB adopted a 'Gujarati culture'—as Shanti puts it—of checking whether there was a business opportunity to make a return. 'This means we are not bankers, we are "Business People", she proclaims. Making a risk-adjusted return is a business attitude built into the culture of the bank, which is first a business. This attitude came to use when it was time to make some hard decisions, especially those relating to its brand and the business of banking.

Uday explains,

> In the initial stage, there was little clarity whether the KMB brand belonged to the Kotak family or to the Kotak Mahindra Group. We first took the clear decision that the bank is not owned solely by the Kotak family. It was a distinct entity and owned the brand 'Kotak', with the logo. So, there would be no brand payment. Straightforward. The Institution owns it and will own it in perpetuity.

Then there was the issue of coming up with a logo symbolic of what they stood for. They chose the Devanagari 'ka', क, for Kotak in Hindi, which was distinctly Indian in its origin, but with the infinity curve, which is universal, thus choosing a logo with a uniquely global Indian personality.

Thinking like a business, technology was another important decision. Kotak had a choice between iFlex and Infosys to set up the banking platform. Mindful of capital at the time, the company went with iFlex, as its quote was lower than Infosys.' However, this was a short-term view and Uday soon realized that a long-term vision was needed. By 2008-09, it was clear that Kotak's equation with iFlex was not working out and it switched to Infosys. Uday learned a lesson that any subsequent change in technology is painful and costly in terms of time.

## THINK INVESTMENTS, THINK KOTAK

As a new bank among established players, Kotak needed to position itself differently from other banking companies. As Uday clarifies the thought that went into this question:

> How do we differentiate ourselves as 'Bank No. 110'? I don't remember the exact number, but we were pretty low down. So, we created a theme. We reasoned that people have known us for our prowess in investment, capital markets and securities. We were also known for our partnership with Goldman. So, we decided to start as a bank that would provide high quality differentiated advice, an idea that was concisely caught in 'Think Investments, Think Kotak.'

With clarity of purpose and a will to differentiate itself, KMB went on to stand out from the pack. Its focus on economic value manifested itself in its market cap. After all, as Shanti reasons,

> The market cap is the outsider's confidence in you and everything you stand for, including your business model, people model, culture, profitability, integrity and just about everything. So, while other firms would have said, 'Double your profits, double your revenues,' we said, 'double your value, because if you start from that, you will do everything right. Another Kotak mantra has been, 'Not volume for volume's sake, unless it is accompanied by economic value.'

Uday concurs KMB's emphasis on economic value and feels that all their decisions were based on the underlying factor of value accretion. As Uday states, 'If something did not create economic value, we would not do it just to boost the next quarter's earnings.'

Uday strongly believes that creative accounting, to make the quarterly numbers look better, does not help. He says,

> For sustainable build-up of value, we are ready to endure pain today in the Profit and Loss statement (P&L), if we make a mistake or lose money. When we entered the credit card business in 2008 for instance, we lost a lot of money, but we took the pain.

This unique business outlook has helped KMB to create investor confidence and trust even as it started its journey, thinking of its brand, logo and positioning to create value, just as any other fast-moving consumer goods (FMCG) business would do. 'After all, we were getting into a consumer business,' Uday quips. Just like a business, expansion is a natural corollary to growth.

## SOARING GROWTH

Despite its conservative outlook, Kotak sought to expand its presence through strategic initiatives. In 2014, KMB acquired the Bengaluru-headquartered ING Vysya Bank in an all-stock deal, making it the fourth largest private bank at the time in terms of total business. The deal helped KMB leverage ING's digital banking strengths, as ING was among the top two or three consumer banks in Germany with zero branch presence, as also its expertise in international corporate banking. It helped KMB ramp-up its branch presence in South India, in a scenario where 46 per cent of KMB's branches were in West India only. The bank was also able to diversify its loan book beyond its own retail loan business, as ING's strength was its small and medium enterprises (SME) clientele. With ING Vysya nearing the foreign shareholding cap of 74 per cent, the merger also yielded more liquidity and significant headroom for foreign money as the foreign shareholding after the merger was 47 per cent. The deal also helped Uday Kotak reduce the promoter's stake in KMB, in line with the roadmap given by the RBI, and move towards the prescribed stake of 30 per cent.[56]

Its number of subsidiaries also grew. In 2004, the Group entered the alternate assets business with the launch of a private equity fund. In 2006, they bought out the stake of

---

[56]'Kotak Buys ING Vysya in All-share Deal.' *Business Standard*, www.business-standard.com/article/companies/kotak-mahindra-bank-to-merge-with-ing-vysya-bank-114112000844_1.html. Accessed 4 July 2020.

Goldman Sachs in both KMCC and Kotak Securities Ltd., before opening the bank's representative office in Dubai. In 2009, they launched a pension fund under the National Pension System. Additionally, in 2014, KMB acquired 15 per cent equity stake in the Multi Commodity Exchange Ltd. of India (MCX).

A few years later, in 2017, KMB announced taking its organic growth strategy through the digital route by launching '811'—a banking app which allowed customers to open an account with zero balance. This app was inspired by the date on which Prime Minister Narendra Modi had announced demonetization—8 November or 8/11. The goal was to try and double the customer base in 18 months and was in fact KMB's response to the disruption in banking. In January 2020, when the RBI amended the Know Your Customer (KYC) norms and introduced the video-based KYC option to on-board customers, KMB was the first bank to integrate the Video KYC process in the account opening journey. This instant banking has been popular among its customers.

## A BANK WITH A HEART

Kotak prides itself on being a 'Bank with a Heart.' Be it with employees or customers, the satisfaction of building personalized relationships is present. This family-like atmosphere manifests itself in Uday knowing at least 50 of his senior team members personally by speaking with them, sending them flowers on their birthdays and even visiting them on special occasions. While this may have to do with Uday's own family business background, Shanti observes,

> These actions are unique to Uday because he cares about others and they are not being done on the advice of a management consultant. I don't send out flowers because I think it is a waste of money. But I do call up people at least three levels below on their birthdays and speak to them.

She admits however that this personal touch has continued due to the presence of the first generation. The challenge would be to retain this in the third generation as well.

The bank, unlike others of its ilk, also promotes an 'open culture' which encourages dissent. The senior team attests to the manner in which Uday has always encouraged them to stand up and challenge him and his decisions, which has influenced them to promote dissent in their teams as well, which Shanti believes is rare in other institutions.

How has Kotak Mahindra Bank managed to position itself as a strong private sector bank and achieve so much in less than two decades? What sets it apart? Is it the conservative outlook befitting a bank, its bold use of technology and being at the forefront of the digital space or just being in the right place at the right time? When asked about this, Uday simply says that the bank's success may be attributed to learning its lessons in time and diligently practicing a set of their own 'Working Principles'. Some of these principles include,

1.  If you don't understand something, don't do it. Simply put, it is better to be stupid now, than to be sorry later.
2.  If something is too good to be true, it usually is.
3.  Take granular steps. You will be slower, but your success will be more solid and sustainable.

4. Keep your culture. Don't pretend to be someone you are not.

5. Communicate freely and work together as a team.

These working principles may well be Uday's success mantras for young entrepreneurs inspired by his success and that of KMB. Additionally, Uday adds, 'You must have passion with purpose, but with loads of common sense to question your passion.' Uday practices what he believes in. For instance, he may have started the bank but it is structured in a way that everything is owned by the bank. 'Uday Kotak does not own anything other than the shares of the bank, so there is no conflict of interest,' Uday states.

Additionally, all Kotak entities are 100 per cent subsidiaries, held by the bank, and the bank is the only listed entity. This is different from some of the other financial institutions (say ICICI) which have separately listed subsidiaries. The reason Kotak decided to buy out all its partnerships and kept them under the bank was, as Uday explains, due to their belief that the value that accrues should go to the holding company shareholder, with the bank being both the operating bank and a holding company.

With values and vision, Uday set up an NBFC, which he successfully transformed into a Scheduled Commercial Bank with 18 subsidiaries, within two decades. Let's now look at some of the characteristics of Shapers that we can discern from Uday's journey in the next chapter.

Chapter 6

# Decoding the Shaper

'If you want to build a ship, don't drum up the
men to gather wood, divide the work, and give
orders. Instead, teach them to yearn for the vast
and endless sea.'

—Antoine de Saint-Exupéry, French writer and aviator

What does it take to lead an NBFC in an era characterized by extreme trust deficit and convert it into a bank before carrying it through a global financial crisis when the working of the entire financial world is suspect? What does it take to create one of India's most valuable banks[57] within 16 years, with 1600 branches and employing more than 60,000 people[58]? Is this the achievement of a charismatic leader or is there something more?

[57]KMB enjoyed a market capitalization of of ₹2,55,537.49 crores, as of 2 April 2019, and was in the third position behind HDFC and ICICI Bank Ltd. in terms of market capitalization in 2019. ('Top 10 Largest Banks in India 2020.' *MyMoneyMantra*, 26 October 2020, www.mymoneymantra.com/blog/these-are-the-top-10-largest-banks-in-india/. Accessed 4 July 2020.)
[58]'Kotak Mahindra Bank Announces Results for Bank PAT and Consolidated PAT FY20.' *Kotak Mahindra Bank*, 13 May 2020, https://www.kotak.com/content/dam/Kotak/about-us/media-press-releases/2020/Media-Release_Q4FY19-20.pdf. Accessed 4 July 2020.

It is our theory, as described in this series of books, that it takes more than a leader to accomplish these tasks successfully and in a seemingly effortless manner. What it takes is a Shaper, who through his Mindset, Behaviour and Actions is able to influence the upward trajectory of the organization, not just etched by financial success, but also by a reputational lead and longevity, which can far outlive its founder or CEO.

The intent of the Shaper series is not just to list out the mindsets, behaviours and actions, but possibly 'humanize' them through anecdotes and stories, that can be easily understood and possibly replicated by others desirous of following this path. In doing so, we believe, we provide invaluable lessons in institution-building.

## HANDPICKING PERSONNEL

To convert a 300 sq ft office space into a dream financial consultancy, required people and then to transform this organization into an institution, required superior-level talent. Not an easy task for any CEO, let alone a 23-year old entrepreneur-founder, a young upstart in a difficult industry going through terrible churn.

Shivaji sums it up succinctly, 'I met Uday for the first time, six months after I started my stint at Nelco. He was so young. I had imagined a much older person, because of the big cheques he used to write.'

Starting from a one-man outfit, with just two lower-level team members, how does one build a thinking, planning outfit with reach? An important step in building a team is to spot talent and then attract it. Uday had a rather unconventional approach to recruiting talent. He has a story about each of the people he hand-picked for the roles at Kotak Mahindra. The common thread across all such recruitments was an eye for noting excellence, recognizing competitiveness and aggression and respecting people who stood for middle-class values.

Shivaji, 'the finance guy at Nelco', was one of the earliest to join Uday in a senior leadership role. Uday had great respect for Nelco, a Tata company and for Shivaji, who would stringently negotiate terms with him on behalf of Nelco.

As Uday narrates,

> We were both young[59] and when I was at Nelco, I was impressed with Shivaji's value system about wanting to protect his company. He would oppose and negotiate for a ₹100 service charge I was trying to add on each bill discounted. Anybody who has been good on the other side, I want to bring them on my side. The day I met Shivaji and interacted with him, I saw he was different, a dreamer with a keen value system. I wanted him.

The story of Shanti joining KMFL in 1991 is also extremely unconventional. She was a truly blue-blooded professional—an A.F. Ferguson[60] chartered accountant working at Bank of Nova Scotia, one of the Indian foreign banks. Uday interacted with Shanti when he went to Bank of Nova Scotia to rediscount the bills of his clients like Nelco or Bharat Forge, which was also a large business for the Bank. Two months after Nova Scotia started to rediscount these bills, Uday was informed that

---

[59]Shivaji and Uday are almost the same age.
[60]A.F. Ferguson is one of the oldest accounting and audit firms of India.

the Bank had gone to Bharat Forge directly. This happened with other companies as well, whose bills Uday had sought to rediscount with Nova Scotia.

Uday recounts the incident,

> Apparently, Shanti had seen the flow of our bills and to do away with us as an intermediary, she went to meet these customers directly. I should have been upset. How can she steal my business? But deep down, it made me more competitive. We stopped giving our Bharat Forge bills to Bank of Nova Scotia. We got another bank that offered us lower rates, but to do business with Nova Scotia, I had to squeeze my margins. Shanti being a feisty fighter was effectively competing with me, and that deeply impressed me. When I confronted her for stealing my customers, she nonchalantly said, 'Yes, but that's my job. I am a bank. I cover all these customers in Mumbai and Pune.'
> I said, 'Fine Shanti, but remember, I've got other banks.'
> I was impressed with her spirit of competitiveness and it was not easy to get her on-board KMFL.

It took Uday four months to convince her. 'After all, she was working at a foreign bank located in a fancy office in Mittal Court at Nariman Point, not in a 300 sq ft office in Navsari building,' he says.

Shanti narrates her story: 'I already had an offer from Deutsche Bank and Standard Chartered when Uday invited me to join him. I asked him, "You already have three chairs in your office. Where do you have space for a fourth chair?" Uday then took me to see his new office at Nariman Bhawan.'

Also, being from a South Indian family, a community known for its risk -aversion, she faced much scepticism from family and friends. 'I was asked, 'Why do you want to move from a foreign bank to an NBFC?'" she recalls. The fact that she still agreed to take up this quasi-entrepreneurial opportunity also speaks of Uday's powers of overcoming opposition.

## A TEAM OF ACHIEVERS

Uday chose his teams carefully. He wanted people who were tough, competitive and had demonstrated their skill. He was also drawn by his respect for certain organizational cultures like those built by Anand Mahindra.

Was he trying to harness opposite polarities while most would seek to build teams comprising of like-minded people? Uday agreed, saying, 'You should be open to doing things which will add to the strength of the firm. This does not necessarily mean restrictively looking at people from certain kinds of organizations, with certain kinds of backgrounds.'

Uday then cites the example of another senior person, Narayan, a chartered accountant, who became part of the KMFL team as financial controller in 1991 and went on to become the CEO of Kotak Securities. He is currently the Head of Treasury in KMB.

Uday narrates Narayan's story,

I was the sole proprietor of my stock broking business, rather upset with a manager who had made a mess of my books of accounts. So, one day I asked Shivaji, 'Do you know a good accountant who can make sure that the books of accounts of my stock broking firm are tallied and reconciled?' Shivaji said, 'Yes. I know this one accountant who works for various people and commutes with me daily on the local train from Chembur to Victoria Terminus (VT). I can bring him here. That fellow was Narayan.

So, Narayan started with me as a consultant to tally the books of my small, insignificant broking business. He was extremely sharp, but he used to work for many customers. After 18 months of working with me, I convinced him to join me.

Among the others who joined him early was C. Jayaram, currently a non-executive director at KMB. Jayaram had joined Uday in 1989. He had a choice of joining Reliance, but decided to go with Kotak. Jayaram ran the car finance business. Then there was K.V.S. Manian, currently a whole time Director on the Board of the Bank along with Dipak Gupta and Gaurang Shah.

Kotak speaks of Manian's 'acquisition' with pride,

Manian started his career with Nelco in the 1980s and had worked with Shivaji, who was extremely keen on bringing him into Kotak. Manian, however, left Nelco to join Premier Auto Electric in the early '90s. We could not get him then, but in 1996, we finally got him. He joined around the same time as Gaurang and Jaimin.

Unlike those who feel threatened by talent among the reporting levels, Uday revels in having teams that comprise 'achievers', who can question, challenge and express dissent. Uday's team then, has typically comprised of people with a certain value system, aggression, competitiveness and yet with high ethical standards and who have brought value to the organization. As Uday says, 'If your team members are better than you, that's what you want.' Further, it was these few people he had hired initially, who in turn employed others like themselves. 'The first 50 got the next 50 and so on,' says Shivaji.

Uday's resolute conviction in the pursuit of top talent to join his fledgling organization in the early days is noteworthy, especially when such talent had joined him, quite clearly, for reasons other than money. It is clear that a Shaper mindset is one which seeks to break barriers and goes about its goals in dogged pursuit, with clear focus and determination.

## LOOKING OUT FOR GOOD PEOPLE

Uday's ability to connect with people at a deeper level and forge relationships that endured time was partly the reason how he could go about effortlessly breaking barriers in pursuit of goals. There are many who can attest to his people skills. Shivaji calls him a 'charmer'—one who is able to persuade others to share his dreams. This sobriquet is not entirely misplaced, because it was not limited to his ability to get talent on board, but may be discerned in his multiple business decisions too. He has this unique ability to almost always have his way, without creating ill-will and rancour in the process.

Uday speaks of the time he managed to draw Jaimin Bhatt from his previous company, Indus Venture Fund, where he worked for T. Thomas and Bipin Shah. Such poaching in a close-knit industry, especially one where talent was scarce, may have been looked at askance. However, Kotak desperately needed someone good in the Finance Department, and Shivaji, 'who was a great one for spotting good people,' figured out that Jaimin was 'a thorough, meticulous and a high-conscience guy.' Just the person they wanted. Shivaji was able to convince Jaimin to move. Thus, Jaimin, a chartered accountant and cost accountant, joined the Kotak Mahindra Group in 1995 and has been with them for the last 25 years.

Then there was Falguni Nayar who joined Kotak and played a key role in its growth. Uday relates the incident with a mischievous twinkle in his eye:

> Dipak had joined us before Falguni. He was from Fergusons Consulting division and knew Kumar Advani, a partner at A.F. Ferguson. In 1993, Kumar hosted a dinner at the Taj Chambers for which I was also invited. By that time Dipak had already joined Kotak Mahindra. At that gathering, Kumar had said in jest, 'Uday you have taken one of my good guys. But I have some other good people. Don't take them. Falguni is here. She is very good.
>
> *What was he really thinking when he said that?* thought Uday. I came back and asked Dipak, 'What do you think of Falguni?'
>
> 'Oh, she is very good,' replied Dipak.
>
> They had been colleagues. So, I asked him, "Should we try for her?"
>
> He said, "Let me talk to her."
>
> Falguni was interested. But before I hired her, I told Kumar, 'I am going to take her.'
>
> He said, 'I don't want to lose her, but if it is good for her career, you can take her.'
>
> Falguni soon joined us.

## PROMOTING EXCELLENCE

This child-like innocence and simplicity in a shrewd businessman, has helped Uday to maintain trusting relationships in the face of tough, strategic calls. Amit Desai, his friend from Sydenham College, and one of India's leading criminal lawyers today, confirms this. He says,

> I can't think of coming across one person in all these years who has disliked Uday. He would always top the university exams. But underlying this feat was a genuine effort to excel, which went beyond the ordinary. He would go and look for books in the library, which others wouldn't access, and then walk that extra mile towards topping his exams. It was only much later, after the results were out, that he would tell us with his mischievous smile what went into being a topper. Nobody grudged him that performance, as Uday is still friends with a large number of people whom he studied with, both at school and in college.

People instinctively trust Uday because he is genuine. For instance, while most might consider getting the Mahindra name early on as a master stroke in branding, Uday reveals, 'There is no piece of [signed] paper between us. It is only based on our relationship. A deep, personal relationship.' In this day and age, for a relationship to last so long can happen only on the basis of mutual trust and deep respect. Uday's trust and regard for this relationship is also evident from the fact that he invited Harish to be the first chairman of KMFL. He continued to be the chairman throughout his lifetime.

In 2017, the Twitter world was witness to their mutual

affection and admiration when Anand tweeted, '1985. Young Uday Kotak enters my office and offers financing. He's so smart, I ask if I can invest in him. My best decision.' This was in response to a news item which stated that KMB had surged ahead of ICICI Bank in terms of market-cap. Uday, in turn, tweeted, 'Thank you Anand. You are my friend, mentor and guide in this journey.'

Beyond identifying and attracting talent, Shapers like Uday are known for their high levels of empathy, which helps in nurturing and retaining talent. Falguni, who had joined Kotak Mahindra in 1993, exemplifies talent who was nurtured to give her best and drive the institution onto a growth path in a completely new trajectory.

Uday speaks of Falguni's stint at Kotak,

> We had started a consulting division in KMFL. A year after she joined us, Sanjay [Nayar], her husband, who was working in Citibank, was posted to London. Like a typical Indian wife, she wanted to join him. So, we took a view. We said, 'Falguni if you go to London, we will set up a London office. We want to do sale and trading in equities and in GDRs. Why don't you set it up?
>
> So, Falguni set up our London office. Kotak Mahindra (UK) happened because of Falguni. After two years, Sanjay was transferred to New York. We said, 'Great! Falguni set up New York.' By then, we had already set up a JV with Goldman. I asked her to work for six months at the Goldman Sachs office. Then we set up our separate office in New York. When Sanjay returned to India as Country Head, Citibank, we brought her back as Head of our equities business in India. She headed

Kotak Investment Banking, a subsidiary of KMB.

In 2012, Falguni told me, 'Uday, I am happy with what I have been doing. I have done well, but I want to do something different. I won't compete with you.' I asked, 'What are you going to do?' She said, 'I am passionate about doing something in Internet and beauty.'

While Kotak was surprised, he understood her need to create something from scratch. That's how Falguni, investment banker, who had traversed continents working with Kotak Mahindra for nearly two decades, started her entrepreneurial venture, Nykaa—the Indian retail outlet of beauty, wellness and fashion products.

Uday's empathy enables him to maintain relationships, even after the employee has left the organization. Shivaji recalls an incident involving Kirit Ashar, one of Kotak's earliest employees, since before even the forging of the KM relationship. Kirit was unwell and bed-ridden in his house in Vashi with jaundice. Uday went to meet him along with Shivaji, despite the long commute between South Bombay, where Uday lived and worked, and Vashi.

'We made him feel comfortable. Uday provided him financial support too. Kirit remembers that even today. Even after working 8-10 hrs, Uday would always manage to touch people by becoming a part of their lives on their special occasions,' Shivaji adds.

In fact, Shivaji recalls how Uday and the entire top brass of Kotak was present at a surprise birthday party that his wife and son had organized for him when he turned 60, two years ago. What touched his heart was the fact that Uday, his wife Pallavi, Jayaram and others from the Kotak team had travelled to Chembur on a working day to be there for him, even though he had retired from the company. He also remembers Uday visiting him in the hospital when he had a surgery one year ago, even though he was travelling to Japan that very night. He also offered to pick up the entire tab for the surgery. It wasn't necessary, but he still did that. These nurturing gestures create a strong social fabric and define the organization,' Shivaji said. Amit also attests to how Uday has quietly helped people, without fuss and fanfare, over the years.

## ORBIT CHANGING FORAYS

A business relationship that Uday had built over a period of time was with Goldman Sachs. The focus and steely resolve that was witnessed while developing the team could be seen once again, when Uday focused on achieving his vision—that of evolving into an Indian financial institution with global class and capabilities. This required an orbit-changing move in terms of seeking a credible international partnership. Uday set his eyes on a JV with Goldman Sachs. A partnership that started off as an agency relationship in 1992, was nurtured and developed into a JV in 1995.

When Goldman wanted a higher stake in the JV, Uday was clear that he was not ready to give more than 25 per cent stake. 'Let us build a business together. I want skin in the game,' Uday responded. When Goldman refused to lend its name to the JV, Uday was unflustered. The Goldman name did not feature in the company name, but Uday called the new entity 'Kotak Capital' and then added: 'JV with Goldman Sachs'. The other JV with Goldman Sachs, Kotak Securities, also involved 25 per cent stake of the foreign partner.

This was unlike what his competitors had chosen to do at the time. Hemendra Kothari, who founded DSP Financial Consultants in 1975 partnered with Merrill Lynch in 1995 to form DSP Merrill Lynch, with Merill getting a 40 per cent stake. Similarly, Nimesh Kampani of JM Financial had entered into a JV with Morgan Stanley to form JM Morgan Stanley in 1997, with the foreign company owning a 49 per cent stake.[61] Uday, unlike his competitors, was unwilling to part with more than 25 per cent stake, citing that an option might be worked out at a future date, at which point attachment of the partner's name could also be sought. Goldman found this arrangement convenient in 1995, as India was an underdeveloped market for them to come in on their own, at the time. They were comfortable with Uday and Kotak Mahindra as partners, based on their diligent norms and their personal relationships.

However, 10 years later, by 2006, the Indian market had changed dramatically. 'India was now hot,' says Uday, referring to the phenomenally high Indian real growth rate of 9.2 per cent per annum in the year, as well as the growth of the financial sector.

Brooks Entwistle, chief executive of Goldman Sachs (India) LLC, had indicated their ambitious India plan in a statement, 'The Indian market represents tremendous growth opportunity, and the group would now look at building an "onshore" presence that is fully integrated with its global businesses.' Goldman therefore sought a higher stake in the JV. When it didn't work out, Kotak Mahindra and Goldman Sachs mutually decided to part ways in March 2006.

---

[61]This JV also ended in 2007, with JM Financial acquiring Morgan Stanley's share.

Uday explains the reason for the separation,

We were ready to move Goldman to 49 per cent. In principle, we had already done a handshake to call it Kotak Goldman with us at 51 and Goldman at 49 per cent. However, Hemendra's deal with Merrill Lynch happened then. Hemendra sold his 57 per cent stake to Merrill Lynch in tranches between 2005-2009, with 50 per cent being sold in 2005 itself.[62] Also, in 2005-06, India became important and Goldman Sachs said, 'Posterity would not forgive us if we were not in control of our destiny.' They wanted to hold the majority stake at 51-49 per cent. We couldn't possibly find an arithmetic, which could allow both of us to own 51 per cent at the same time. So, we decided to charter our own destiny.

Uday was willing to buy out Goldman's stake irrespective of the price at which it could happen. KMB bought out Goldman Sachs' 25 per cent stake each in KMCC and Kotak Securities for ₹333 crore in 2006.

## BEING SWADESHI

The parting was amicable, a testament to the supreme people relations which Uday has been known for. 'We parted as friends. The relationship is good even today, but interests differ. You just have to do what is right,' Uday avers. In fact, Goldman Sachs was the banker for Kotak's capital issuance

---

[62]'Merrill Buys out Kothari in DSP.' *The Financial Express*, 9 December 2005, www.financialexpress.com/archive/merrill-buys-out-kothari-in-dsp/156862/. Accessed 4 July 2020.

in May 2020.

Uday does admit that the decision to part ways with Goldman was indeed difficult, but he has no regrets. 'The core team discussed this and we decided it was about doing what was right for our destiny, our future. We could not continue in the minority, as merely an investor,' he states simply.

Kotak's priorities were clear. As Dipak states, 'Goldman was willing to give us a crazy amount of money for the deal. However, we were clear. For us, being minority was as good as being zero. It didn't work. That's when we bought them out.'

The other JV with Ford had already come to an end in 2005, because Kotak would finance cars from other manufacturers, and the foreign partner did not want to support non-Ford products and dealers.

Shivaji says of this phase, 'At the time, many people in the organization felt that we would not do well without our foreign partners, but we bought out both Ford Credit and Goldman. There was pride in India and being an Indian.' His explanation for Kotak's parting of ways with its foreign partners is, 'At heart, Uday is Swadeshi.'

Kotak's confidence and conviction regarding its priorities set it apart and defined it as an institution. As Jayaram says,

India was our playground. So, there was no reason why we couldn't do it ourselves, with our own expertise. We didn't need to sell out to the foreign players. This may sound fashionable now, but in the late '90s, it was more common to sell. I believe that is what defined us as an institution.

## CRITICAL THINKING

Uday's clear sense of priorities has enabled him to meticulously consider every option and weigh the pros and cons of each before arriving at a decision. When Kotak decided to go international and a deal with Goldman Sachs was struck, for instance, Uday was clear about how to give equity to foreigners. Explaining his decision, he points out that equity was given away in the subsidiaries—Kotak Securities, Kotak Capital and Kotak Mahindra Primus, but not in KMFL, the parent company. The influx of capital by the partner meant that Kotak actually capitalized the subsidiaries through the JVs, in which the parent company had put little money. The JV with Goldman was the result of the personal relationships they had struck with Hank Paulson. It was in 1996, that interest rates in India were spiking sharply. However, the capital from both the JVs—Goldman and Ford— came in just before the interest rates spiked, which provided Kotak Mahindra with the shock-absorbing capacity through tougher times.

## BEING PARANOID

'Only the paranoid survive,' stated Andy Grove, former CEO of Intel, which is an apt description for Uday's business acumen. By 1996, the interest rates in India were fluctuating between 18 per cent and 20 per cent. The RBI governor, Dr Rangarajan had increased the interest rates dramatically and was keeping liquidity tight. In 1997, finance companies started mushrooming all over India and people were raising money through 17 per cent debentures for five and nine years. Kotak

Mahindra was witnessing initial pangs in its loan portfolio and balance sheet.

In mid-1997, just before the Asian crisis, Uday had an epiphanous moment, when sensing serious trouble ahead, he called in his senior managers and told them, 'I am willing to bet that in one year's time, 99 per cent of these finance companies will go bust. I want you to stop going out and looking for business. In fact, I want to shrink our lending by 50 per cent.'

At that time, KMFL's loan book was ₹1,800 crore. The company, on Uday's strictures, got out of ₹800 crore worth of loans and actually cut its limits because they felt that this couldn't last. Uday could see that the financial sector was likely to go into serious defaults. So, he pruned his balance sheet by design.

As it turned out, it was the right thing to do. As credit was squeezed, the financial sector faced its biggest ever crisis. Out of the 4000 non-bank financial services company in India in 1997, only 20 survived. Kotak was one of the companies which weathered the storm.

Uday recollects,

We were saved because we cut down our exposure. We still lost about 10 per cent of our portfolio, which was large, but imagine the loss if we had expanded our portfolio from ₹1,800 crore, as others did. Nobody saw it coming, not even financial institutions like IDBI, IFCI, etc. We hunkered down on our lending book. I told my people to just focus on equity and not on the return on equity, meaning keep your capital in place. That's why we survived that phase with our net worth intact.

Overall, we took a hit of ₹100 crore in bad debts, but by then, we were strong enough to manage.

In an interview in 2010, when Uday was asked what made him reduce his balance sheet at the time when everyone was expanding theirs, Uday provides an answer, which again provides a peek into the Shaper's mindset,

I think there are two sides to my personality. At one level, I like scaling up and I want to expand. But I am also a very conservative and cautious person. There is this constant conflict between these two contradictory personality traits. In this case, the conservative part of me won. I kept thinking that if Unit Trust of India (UTI) was in trouble, the government would bail it out. But nobody was going to bail out Kotak. So, that paranoia probably saved us.

This episode actually started another maxim within the company, which is popular and oft-quoted, 'Return of Capital is more important than Return on Capital.'

This cautious approach saved Uday, but also cost him initially in terms of public perception. He recalls, 'Most people thought we were stupid. Our share price had shrunk to ₹16 in 1997.'[63] Uday faced one Agni-Pariksha after another in the 1990s, but while the shareholders lost money, it was clear that stakeholder consideration reigned supreme in Uday's mind when making these contrarian decisions.

It is such a mindset that is dominated by people relations, critical thinking, opportunity-seizing, orbit-changing and

---

[63]Remember, the share had been listed at ₹1300 in 1992.

stakeholder-oriented behaviour, focus and determination, which set Uday Kotak apart from his peers as a Shaper. It also helped in shaping the Institution into a financial powerhouse, as we shall see in the next chapter.

Chapter 7

# Creating A Financial Powerhouse

'Do not judge me by my success,
judge me by how many times I fell
down and got back up again.'

—Nelson Mandela, former President of South Africa

Organizations which go through repeated Trials by Fire are akin to gold which goes through fire to emerge brighter, purer and stronger from the exercise. While gold is used to make lustrous jewellery, such organizations withstand the trials and tribulations and gradually transform into Institutions. But what is that X-factor that enables these organizations to withstand such trials—that which segregates them from the rest and mandates their transformation into institutions that are long-lasting, trusted and respected among all categories of stakeholders. Their reputation is aspirational for others within the industry.

The story of Uday and KMB reinforces learnings from other shapers and institutions. 'Institutions' are about the 4Ps—people, clarity of purpose, knit through processes and salient work policies that motivate performance. While this remains a common theme, it is the stories about these 4Ps shared across our Shaper Institutions which may differ. Even so, these stories retain the strong undertones of a Shaper at work, moulding and integrating each of these elements, almost into a dough which, given time, ferments, rises and voilà, takes the shape of an institution!

## BECOMING A MEGALITH

Dipak speaks of the growth of the Kotak Mahindra Group in five phases. Phase One spanned over the first five to six years and comprised Uday working with as few as three, to as many as, 100 people, essentially carrying out bill discounting. The product was needed, the environment was suitable and it did well. Phase Two started from the public issue of KMFL in 1992 and went on up to the NBFC crisis of 1997-98, a period that featured two key JVs and the group's own entrepreneurship. This phase formed the bedrock of institution building. Phase Three was from 1998 till the acquisition of the banking license in 2003, which was the time of consolidation, when the group entered both banking and insurance. Phase Four was marked by the time leading up to the global financial crisis in 2008, characterized by all round growth following the bull run in the capital markets that did very well. Phase Five, the decade starting from the financial crisis and onwards, is marked by actual institution building following the learnings post the crisis and strengthening of convictions. During this phase, the two JV partners broke away and the Kotak Mahindra group was on its own. The later part of this phase was characterized by Kotak's entry into digital banking alongside traditional banking, and included products like the 811 digital savings accounts.

The Group itself is a megalith today, comprising 18 subsidiaries under KMB, spread out in asset management, insurance, non-bank, stressed assets and investment banking businesses. These subsidiaries are Kotak Securities, Kotak Mahindra Capital Company (KMCC), Kotak Mahindra Prime, Kotak Mahindra Asset Management Company, Kotak Investment Advisors, Kotak Mahindra Investments, Kotak Mahindra Life Insurance Company, Kotak Mahindra General Insurance Company, Kotak Mahindra Trustee Company, Kotak Mahindra Trusteeship Services, Kotak Mahindra Pension Fund, Kotak Mahindra (International), Kotak Mahindra (UK), Kotak Mahindra Inc., Kotak Mahindra Asset Management (Singapore) Pte Limited, Kotak Infrastructure Debt Fund, Ivy Product intermediaries and BSS Microfinance.

We have explored these phases of transformation in the earlier chapters. Let's now look at the ingredients that shaped the creation of the institution through these phases.

## INVITING TALENT: I WANT, I GET!

'I thought this guy is so good; why don't I get him here?' Uday makes this statement, almost matter-of-factly, referring to most of the people he had recruited and who went on to become the backbone of the Kotak Mahindra Group over the years.

It is a simple statement that may otherwise attract no attention, except that it was made by a 25-year-old, in an industry suspicious of any new-comer, especially one so young. And get them he did, with dollops of personal charm, grit and determination to build an Indian financial powerhouse!

However, the moot question remains, what made these intelligent, young, pedigreed professionals, give up well-paying, cushy jobs in blue-blooded organizations and not only work with Uday, but stay with him for their entire career! Most of the senior management of Kotak Mahindra Group like Shivaji, Gaurang, Dipak, Jayaram, Shanti, Jaimin and others have spent 20 to 30 years—their entire careers—with the organization. The other question is: how did they contribute to the making of an institution?

The second question is easier to answer. A group of talented, young individuals led by a passionate, determined leader— almost their own age—create a culture, which binds and bonds them as they make sense of the madness around, react and respond in bonhomie, trust and strong personal accountability. In the process, they create a valuable bank in terms of market capitalization,[64] second only to another Shaper Institution in this series, HDFC Bank. In June 2020, KMB enjoyed a market cap of ₹255463 crore, as opposed to HDFC Bank's market cap of ₹566926 crore.[65]

The significance of this achievement increases when one looks at another metric such as the price to book value, an indicator of the return a company earns on its assets. In May 2020, KMB pipped all lenders *in the world* to become the most expensive bank stock—a position which until recently belonged to HDFC Bank.[66] Thus, KMB's price-to-book value

---

[64]The market capitalization refers to the value of a company that is traded on the stock market, calculated by multiplying the total number of shares by the share price.

[65]'Kotak Mahindra Bank Market Capital.' *Business Standard*, 19 June 2020, https://www.business-standard.com/company/kotak-mah-bank-2330/peer-comparison/marketcap/bse/sector-by-sector. Accessed 4 July 2020.

[66]'Kotak Mahindra is Now Most Expensive Bank Stock In world.' *The Financial Express*, 22 May 2020, www.financialexpress.com/market/kotak-mahindra-emerges-as-most-expensive-bank-stock-in-world/1966850/. Accessed 4 July 2020.

(P/BV), according to Bloomberg data, was 4.5 times compared with 2.7 times for HDFC Bank and 1.6 times for ICICI Bank.[67] Interestingly, among the 40 biggest lenders globally, two of our Shaper Institutions—Kotak Mahindra Bank and HDFC Bank in addition to ICICI Bank from India—feature among the top six most expensive bank stocks. Kotak is also among the top 10 most valuable companies in India.

This success impacted the senior-level executives who not only invested their careers in Kotak, but became its stakeholders. They have today made it to the list of multi-millionaire Kotakites. All of them came into Kotak as 'Invited Employees,' rather than 'Appointed Employees,' a term Gaurang attributes to one of the earlier HR consultants at KMFL. While Uday 'invited' the first lot, they in turn invited the outstanding talent they came across in their professional lives—to become a part of the Kotak Mahindra growth story.

Gaurang himself speaks fondly of how Shivaji, whom he had met in a professional capacity, had invited him to join 'Kotaaak'—as Shivaji pronounces it—in December 1994. Gaurang did not want to burden Kotak Mahindra with his salary costs while its Ford JV was stuck and even took a 45 per cent cut in the salary he drew. Shanti similarly speaks of her journey that started even before she joined, when her role at the Bank of Nova Scotia involved her haggling with Uday for more than half an hour for 5 to 10 basis points every morning. She too gave up a foreign bank to join an NBFC.

---

[67]The price to book ratio measures the market's valuation of a company relative to its book value. It is given by P/BV= Market price per share/ Book Value per share, where the book value per share is calculated as (Total Assets -Total Liabilities)/ number of shares outstanding.

## THE X FACTOR

Why did they join? Especially when Kotak Mahindra was not really known to be the best paymaster in the industry although its Employee Stock Ownership Plan (ESOP) did help to bridge the gap in the long run.

Dipak speaks about the middle-class values of the current senior management team. When they joined, money was not the main motivating factor. It was the respect they received and some unknown, indescribable X factor. Uday understood the human being and what motivated them. Uday invited Shivaji, a creative person, to 'join him in create something worthwhile.' Shivaji says, 'I was from the middle-class, full of idealism. We wanted to create something with a sense of passion, purpose and some excitement.' The promise of 'continuous learning' was an attraction and contributed to the retention of talent.

All of them, Gaurang, Shivaji, Shanti and others we spoke with, attested to the fact that they did very different things when they joined Uday than they had done in the past. There was a thrill and excitement, exploring new opportunities on this journey, especially in the earlier years. Even the mindset of this handpicked talent was enterprising, willing to march forward and undertake the uncommon. Even if they had never done it before, they were willing to give it a go. Diversity in professional roles and horizontal growth, according to both Jayaram and Dipak, provided the adrenaline rush and kept the learning alive.

This spirit of taking on new roles helped in institution building. As Gaurang recalled,

After I had agreed to join Kotak Mahindra, Dipak called me for a chat to Cricket Club of India (CCI). We walked for about 10 minutes. Then Dipak hesitantly informed me that there had been some change in my job description. I would need to handle the new car financing business upon joining.

Gaurang could not understand what the fuss was about, and says laughingly, 'I thought to myself, you don't need to call me here for saying this. I was after all joining the group and not a particular business.' This attitude that they were part of the group and not of a particular business percolated through the organization and was absorbed by the senior management group.

Jaimin recollects how he joined Kotak in 1995. Even as he started managing proprietary investments, Shivaji came over one day and asked him to help him in the new JV with Ford Credit. In less than six months, it was time for another change when he was asked to explore private equity with Goldman. As it was still early days, the idea of private equity was given up for sometime and he was asked to handle the Mergers and Acquisitions (M&A) business. An additional responsibility of Primary Dealer activity followed, before he moved on to the corporate centre when the NBFC got into banking.

Shanti too looks back at her almost 30-year old career with Kotak Mahindra with satisfaction. She relates the team's zeal to take on new roles with Kotak's growth story. She says for Kotak, while the 1990s were about an entrepreneurial culture, the millennial decade was the seeding of an institution and the period from 2010 has been about scaling and processes, to build an institution. What remained a constant was the call from Uday to enter unchartered territories and take up unexplored roles. 'We just jumped in and accepted these challenges whole-heartedly,' she said. This is as true about her latest role, as head of consumer banking, which Uday asked her to take up in 2014 after an 11-year-long stint as President of Corporate and Investment Banking at KMB.

Equally inspiring is the story of Manian, who joined without any experience in banking or financial services. However, in January 2001, Manian was put in charge of the banking project and played a pivotal role in the conversion of the NBCC into a bank. In 2003, Manian was made head of consumer banking, where the bulk of investments as a bank were made. In April 2014, Uday again took a non-text book banking decision and swapped Manian's and Shanti's roles. Shanti moved from Corporate to retail and Manian to corporate. Manian now heads and oversees the Corporate Banking, Wealth Management, Investment Banking and Institutional Equities businesses.

## PROFESSIONAL ENTREPRENEURS

Uday and KMB embody three attributes that most people value: the opportunity to learn, empowerment and ownership. Each of the senior management team we had interviewed said, 'I had no idea how to do this. But I just got into the role and did it.' As Shanti puts it, 'It was a culture based on no fear of exploring opportunities, available in plenty in the 1990s, complete freedom to operate and innovate even while making mistakes, never taking no for an answer, a street-fighter attitude with real hunger and passion to make it to the top.'

Shivaji seconds this. 'Many of us imagined the business,

created and ran it with support from Uday and guidance from the central team. Maybe funding came from a central team, but all the rest came from this cadre of recruits who were entrepreneurs in their own right.'

Uday's magnetic ability to attract professional talent despite the 300 sq ft office and to instill in them a fierce loyalty to both the brand and the person behind it boils down to his trust in the talent, people development and empowerment. As Uday says,

> This belief in people is rooted in my joint family culture; that you need a strong partnership. I also learned from Goldman, a partnership firm, on how partners work together. It wasn't even a company. It was unlisted. Yet, their systems and their levels of communication were fantastic. Goldman had a crazy voicemail system which used to work 24×7. Each partner used it to keep the other partners informed. Learning from the Goldman culture reinforced many of my family business values that translated into creating a partnership culture in running the firm. While we could not promise too much of money, what we could promise was a concept we later institutionalized: The idea of professional entrepreneurship. Pure professionals or pure entrepreneurs will find the going difficult. So, everyone in this firm is a professional and an entrepreneur.

## FREEDOM TO WORK

This cadre of professional entrepreneurs welcomed the opportunity to create something new. It valued the autonomy and freedom to an extent where they did not join rival banks that offered better perquisites and compensation. Dipak elaborated,

> For most of us, individually, we weren't so much concerned about money alone. We were lucky the organization grew phenomenally horizontally, and there were plenty of opportunities for doing new things, handling new businesses and growth. There was also reasonable independence. Moreover, after a point, we are a family where there are both positives and negatives, and on the balance, the positives far outweigh the negatives, making you stick on.

The freedom that the talent team enjoyed generated a sense of ownership. Shivaji explains, 'With the space and autonomy that was given, we created self-accountability. I would work like it was for my own organization and not as though for somebody else. A large number of people felt that.'

He provides another interesting explanation, 'In any organization, there are promoters, co-promoters and professionals. In this organization, we were able to make many think of themselves as co-promoters.' He also credits 'fairness' as an important trait for an institution to possess, saying Kotak was by and large a fair organization, which is what made people stay. This was built through Uday and the senior management team being approachable—both personally and professionally.

It was also an organization where most people came from similar backgrounds. Gaurang, for instance, speaks of the shared culture among KMB employees, which manifested in simple shared traits like coming from a middle-class background, having common values, caring for parents, staying with them, etc. The bonhomie and trust built with each other through a long association with the organization was reflected in positive peer-ratings, as compared to other organizations, where peers are usually perceived as competitors. It also meant this group was not only of colleagues at work, but also friends at the personal level, with families getting together regularly to celebrate life. Building such team spirit and culture in any organization largely depends on the top leadership, which values the team above the individual. Uday was successful at ensuring this critical ingredient of institution building.

## UNWRITTEN CONVICTIONS

Most institutions we have studied, have been obsessive about processes. Kotak Mahindra stands out as an organization, where, despite the apparent lack of detailed manuals listing out processes and standard operating procedures, especially in the early days before the formation of the bank, there was a code of conduct and processes which were ingrained in the organizational culture.

The senior management team speaks of this unspoken code of conduct and credits the JVs, especially Ford Credit, for their early exposure to processes and control mechanisms that were not a part of the Kotak Mahindra DNA and were often mocked at by them. As Dipak says with a smile,

> Our office was in Bakhtawar Towers, a 14 storey commercial building on Marine Drive. We would joke that if there was a fire in Bakhtawar, what would

Mr. Gosling, the Managing Partner at Ford, do? The process was clearly written down. He would first inform Australia, the regional headquarters, then Detroit, the global headquarters, then the MD because that is the process. If, by then, the fire hadn't spread wildly, he could inform the Fire Department.

Dipak however, credits the two JVs with Goldman and Ford for greatly helping in their institution building activities, by providing the exposure to world-class systems, protocols, processes and controls.

Shivaji provides an instance of a basic process that was subsequently incorporated in the Kotak culture, 'While the Kotak Mahindra credit guy would say, "I have spoken to the client. He will return next week," the Ford Credit guy would say, "Note it in the software."'

Kotak however, followed some unwritten processes, pertaining to almost every activity within the organization, that Dipak terms as their 'convictions'. An important approach that Dipak, Shanti and Gaurang attested to was with regard to credit, where the lowest common denominator was taken to prevail. So, if three people had to take a decision on making a loan and if even one person was uncomfortable, they would decline.

Another 'conviction' was the non-reversal of decisions taken above a certain level. Uday himself attests to this as does the senior management team. Thus, as Gaurang says, 'If the credit committee had rejected a particular credit application, it would not get overturned by someone higher up, unless collectively, there was some deliberation based on new information available.'

In the early pre-banking days, the entrepreneurial culture meant little attention to drawing of structures and processes. It was a restless bunch, eager to conquer, that viewed processes as bureaucratic and a hindrance. However, guided by values and convictions, they were clear that if you cannot put it down on paper, don't do it. These implicit rules or 'folklore', as Gaurang calls it, provided the glue in the absence of manuals. Moreover, these unwritten processes helped Kotak survive the 1997 NBFC crisis.

## TRANSFORMATION BRINGS PROCESSES

Yet change was inevitable and following its transformation into a bank, KMB started to pay greater attention to systems, processes and compliance. Although, this path had its cons— restrictions on flexibility, binding in terms of processes and statutory requirements such as the CRR, SLR and priority lending norms, it was decided that transforming into a larger financial institution was in line with its vision, as banks enjoyed maximum credibility. Today, KMB is almost obsessive about compliance with norms and procedures. With processes came structure.

Becoming a bank brought about a dramatic transition from the flat organizational structure of the 1990s. As Gaurang explained, in 2000, an operating managing committee consisting of eight to 10 people was formed. In 2005, a 27-member Kotak Leadership Team (KLT) was formed. This team used to meet with the senior management twice a year, once with family. The KLT was later expanded to 43 members, and after the ING Vysya merger, the number of members in the KLT increased to 55. The Op Man committee was also transformed into the Executive Board and expanded. It is now called Group Management Committee. Currently, following the formalization of such structures, each subsidiary as a strategic business unit, has its own Executive Committee and organizational structure.

A formal organizational structure has helped to streamline operations, structure decision-making and boost employee performance, although the buck still stops at Uday. Yet, Kotak as an institution does not exactly follow the rules prescribed by management gurus when it comes to dealing with performance, having evolved its own way to institutionalize performance.

## INSTITUTIONALIZING PERFORMANCE

As an organization, KMB promotes a culture of performance which permeates through seeing people in action and through resolution of conflict. Gaurang speaks about Uday leading by action. He says, 'If you sent a mail to 10 people, Uday would always be among the top three to respond.'

At performance evaluation meetings, the feedback can be extremely critical, with Uday personally leading the discussions. These team meetings, which the institution has evolved as part of its culture, involve a large number of people from lower levels as well, which in a way helps in transmission of culture. Thus, as Dipak says, 'If the discussion is about consumer banking, Uday would meet not just Shanti, but also twelve of her second level and say five of the third level, once every month or at least once every quarter.'

As Uday has worked in all these roles, he knows exactly what to expect and can immediately assess shortfalls and is brutally honest in his criticism, no matter who it may be. Gaurang speaks about how Uday openly defies HR management theories about 'criticizing in private and praising in public', 'He doesn't care for that. Probably it is his joint family background, which knows how to build and maintain a high Emotional Quotient (EQ), even while it goads people to give their best, the necessary foundation for which is bonhomie and trust,' he says.

Dipak too mentions how Uday has both the passion and the humility to scold someone in public, and yet pick up the phone and apologize for being harsh. On a lighter note, Jayaram states that it 'doesn't help' that Uday has an elephantine memory. He narrates an anecdote:

> When we were exiting the Goldman Sachs JV in 2005-06, I was involved in the negotiation. One of the guys representing Goldman was an Indian from Hong Kong. We learnt that his father was George Fernandes, the erstwhile Defence Minister. Now, Uday's mentor, Sidney Pinto, who had socialist leanings, had introduced him to George, a socialist himself. Uday had visited George's house on a few occasions. So, when we met his son, Uday informed him, 'I know your father. I still remember his residence telephone number,' and rattled off the number. That guy was completely blown away.
>
> So, when he asks us for the numbers in our meetings, we just tell him, 'Uday, you know the numbers. Whatever you say, we will go along with that.'

The Kotak organizational culture also underscores the importance of risk management, which takes precedence.

No one is encouraged to take risks which spell institutional doom, even if it means short-term gains. At the same time, performance is enhanced through the freedom to make mistakes. '"*Zabaan ki baat*" or staying committed to what you have promised is important,' says Shivaji. There is no backing out once something has been promised, even if means underwriting some losses.

Performance is important and it seeps through the institutional DNA. So, neither Kotak Mahindra nor Uday himself have had to remove anyone for non-performance. In fact, KMB is almost like Japanese organizations, promoting life-long associations. It is actually the self-accountability, which translates into a culture of performance that has created the world's most valued bank.

In the process, these individuals, together with Uday, have created tremendous wealth for all stakeholders, including themselves. Over the last two decades, the bank has created many multi-millionaire employees, with five of the bank's top executives[68] currently estimated to own shares worth more than ₹100 crore each. Also, with a wealth of $10.4 billion USD, Uday is counted as one of India's top five billionaires in 2020.[69]

The Kotak Group is expected to create many more multi-millionaires in the next phase of its growth. All the 2000 high

---

[68]These include Shanti Ekambaram, Jaimin Bhatt, Dipak Gupta, Narayan S.A. and Gaurang Shah. ('Meet Multi-millionaire Kotakites: 5 Executives Worth Rs 100 Crore Each in Kotak Bank.' *Business Today*, 28 May 2020, www.businesstoday.in/sectors/banks/meet-multi-millionaire-kotakites-5-top-executives-who-own-shares-worth-rs-100-crore-kotak-bank/story/405202.html.)

[69]Karmali, Naazneen. 'India's 10 Richest Billionaires In 2020.' *Forbes*, 8 April 2020, www.forbes.com/sites/naazneenkarmali/2020/04/07/indias-10-richest-billionaires-in-2020/#557026457c23.

potential employees are mid-management trainees from the '90s, participating in new expansion and growth.

## TRANSCENDING GENERATIONS

An institution is one which sustains through multiple generations and lives beyond its founder and CEOs. Will KMB last long enough? 'I have always held a deep belief that an institution like a bank must live forever. If what you have created does not outlive you, then you have failed. It is the true test of what you are building. It is similar to institutions like Goldman Sachs and Merrill Lynch. Individuals may be the driving force at a point of time. But the institutional framework must be built to sustain beyond individuals,' Uday states with conviction.

Truly, an organization starts with the initial set of people who constitute the cohort, which lays down the structure and beliefs. Thereafter, it is values, culture and the deep DNA, which must percolate down to the last employee. Today, the institution is 70,000 people strong and getting the culture to seep in deeper into the organizational DNA is the key work before it. To make an institution unique, Uday believes it is more about the spirit than about the letter.

'What is the compass by which decision making should be made in a bank or any other firm? When there is a doubt between letter and spirit, let spirit prevail,' Uday explains.

It is a testimony to the shaper that the institution has created enormous personal and institutional wealth for its stakeholders and in doing so, it has created its own manual of success, what we call the Kotak Way, which is what we turn to next.

# Chapter 8

# The Kotak Way

There is such complete alignment between the institution, Kotak Mahindra Bank and its founder Uday Kotak that it extends to its senior management too. They have imbibed the Kotak culture so deeply that they tend to think and behave similarly, much like Uday himself. So, just like in the other books in the Shapers' series that list out all the elements unique to the institution, we were convinced to think of and posit what we call the 'Kotak' way, which is essentially a bunch of convictions, which provides the essential binding thread, and becomes part of the Kotak folklore through actions seen and then relayed.

## TENETS OF THE KOTAK WAY

1. *Dream Big*: Uday's friends from college speak about Uday's dream of wanting to set up a large financial institution in India, which they all used to laugh at. While the inspiration was global, the ways and means of doing it was Indian, even as the global was used to first learn and drive excellence. Whether it was driving a JV with Ford, a 75-year-old blue blooded credit company, taking on mighty Citi in car finance, getting another global

company Goldman Sachs to undertake its first JV in the world, transforming from an NBFC into a bank—the first one to do so or even refusing 'crazy' money to buy out three global JVs, Kotak personifies Uday's achievements through dreaming big and having the conviction to even hold out against the established players.

2. *Empowering Ownership*: At Kotak, professionals are respected for their decisions, allowed to make mistakes, grow personally and nurture the institution in the process. Everyone we spoke to told us that to work at Kotak was to work as though it was their own organization. The training ground that Kotak provided encouraged some of them, like Falguni, to explore their own entrepreneurial skills through new ventures. Very few of the senior management chose to opt out into competitor companies. Such empowerment and the feeling of ownership has been strengthened further through highly valuable ESOPs, which has transformed the personal status of several Kotakites.

3. *Building Consensus*: The feeling of ownership is further enhanced through decision-making, involving consensus building. As most of them attest, most decisions may have already been taken by Uday, but an important Kotak way is to build consensus and get everybody on the same page. Discussions are conducted till the last objection gets resolved. It is quite another matter that sometimes people are so tired, they cave in and say let's just go home, as Jayaram puts it mischievously.

Decision making at Kotak may be 'collective, but comes loaded with veto' power. As Dipak said, the decision-making process is bottom up, rather than top down. 'The bottom has to agree. Then I have a veto to disagree. But if the bottom does not agree, I cannot disagree. I will never override or overrule such disagreement at the bottom level,' he explains emphatically. This system has been proven to work better in the long run even though it may have led to the loss of certain lucrative opportunities in the past. 'About three out of 10 opportunities,' says Dipak putting a number to it. However, they say the Kotak way is, 'We are absolutely fine with it.'

4. *Conservative about Risk*: Being a financial company, Kotak's outlook towards risk sets it apart from others. There is complete clarity on business opportunities, for instance, in terms of what is wrong, what is not wrong and what is grey. It treads cautiously in the grey areas, taking recourse to legal counsel at every step.

Uday has taken risk, but managed it well. Giving up the pursuit of growth to concentrate on consolidating the business depicts his risk outlook. He draws an analogy from the game of tennis, and says, 'When you hit the ball hard, it could either go out of the court, where you have clearly lost a point, or it could be on the line, in which case it can be interpreted either way. What we are clear about is that we will hit the ball well within the line, so that there is no cause for misinterpretation.'

Dipak constantly uses the term Finance 101. He says it boils down to not straying from the knowledge of the basic principles of finance. These learnings have been painfully distilled through experience and through being keen observers of the goings-on in the industry. As Shanti puts it, 'The NBFC crisis was a trial by fire that helped us learn about the credit business, and how lending could wipe you out.'

5. *Living by Letter and Spirit*: Another cultural legacy within Kotak is the distinction between letter and spirit, with priority of spirit over letter. This manifests itself in the way the bank views its social responsibility as well. Shivaji set up the Kotak Education Foundation for the Kotak family, way back in 2006, long before CSR had become mandatory in India. It was in the spirit of philanthropy, characteristic of most traditional Indian business families. When the CSR requirements became mandatory, Kotak Education Foundation was brought under the ambit of Kotak Mahindra Bank. The Bank is committed to the education of the poor and the under-privileged.[70]

For KMB, CSR is more than just a legal compliance. As Uday says, 'It is again a matter of spirit over letter as we want to ensure that the money is well used, and it is not merely to tick a legal box.' Accordingly, the institution has created a three-year CSR plan, where, in addition to the Kotak Education Foundation, the bank will also support a badminton academy by Pulella Gopichand. The bank has started to invest in this academy with a commitment of about ₹40 crore.

6. *Corporate Governance Rules*: Given that the financial

---

[70]They have set up a second independent foundation, the Kotak Family Foundation. This has been started by Uday's younger son, Dhaval, who is passionate about social entrepreneurship. This is owned, overseen by the Kotak family, and Dhaval currently is responsible for it. About 10,000 street kids are fed everyday through this Foundation, and the dream is to feed a million kids a day.

sector is based on trust, it is critical to follow the principles of corporate governance. This is Uday's conviction that has permeated down within Kotak as part of its culture. Belonging to a business family, Uday realized early on, the significance of family relationships coming in the way of doing sound business. He has therefore steadfastly maintained an arms-length distance between business and family, almost to the point of obsession.

This has become an essential part of Kotak's culture. As Jayaram recalls, 'The 2011 Cricket World Cup Final was supposed to be played between India and Sri Lanka at Wankhede Stadium in Mumbai.' Kotak Mahindra had bought a box for the match, to be used for key clients. Jayaram, who was handling the event at the time, had been besieged by calls asking for tickets. He had bought tickets in the lower stands as well for good measure so that they could entertain all their clients' requests. A week before the final match, he received a call from Uday, who hesitantly informed him that he had a peculiar problem. His elder son, Jay, who was studying in the US at the time, had expressed his desire to come to India to watch the finals. Uday asked Jayaram if he could procure tickets in the lower stands for Jay. Jayaram was quite surprised and said that Jay could always have the box. Uday, however, was extremely embarrassed at the very suggestion. He insisted that Jayaram get only one ticket in the lower stands. And sure enough, Jay watched the cricket finals from the lower stands on 2 April 2011.

It is Uday's obsession with propriety that ensured that the company had a Board guiding it on corporate governance since its inception. Uday attributes this learning to the mentoring and guidance he received from Sidney Pinto.

The Mahindras, who started out as promoters of Kotak Mahindra Bank, have remained largely aloof from the day to day running of the bank. Anand also completed his eight-year stint as a Director in 2011. Anand's wife, Anuradha is the only significant shareholder in KMB with a 1.12 per cent stake and that too in the public shareholder category.[71]

7. *Doing 'Right'*: This conviction of doing the right thing is critical to Uday. Be it people relations or sticking on the right side of the law, the idea of doing what is legally and morally right has seeped down as part of the Kotak culture.

As Shivaji states, 'Uday spends a lot of time thinking about doing the right things and in the right way. Finally, he takes a decision which is right for the larger stakeholder.'

Considering that JV partings can turn out to be ugly and acrimonious, Uday's parting from his partners has always been friendly, be it with Goldman Sachs, Ford Credit or Old Mutual.

To explain the secret sauce underlying his amicable exits, Uday uses an analogy from sport. 'When you are in a kite-flying battle and need to cut the string of another kite flyer, you need to first pull to cut the string, but you also need to give *dheel* or let it go slightly. This works in

---

[71]'Out of the ordinary.' *Business India*, 2-15 January 2017, http://www. businessindiagroup.com/download/Kotak-CF.pdf, p. 32. Accessed 4 July 2020.

negotiations too. At times you are pulling the cart hard or you are giving it *dheel*. However, in the entire negotiation process, when what you do is morally right and you have the conviction that what you want and what you ask is the right thing, then it is only a little bit about money here or there and the chances are, you are going to come out right. So, you have to use that moral rectitude and position in spirit strongly in your negotiation.' Perhaps this ability to extricate oneself without acrimony is a characteristic of a Shaper

8. *Agility for Opportunities*: While Kotak is conservative in the way it does business, it has been adept at reading and interpreting the business environment, and moving in and out of critical business situations with agility. It was this ability to spot opportunities that sowed the seeds of an institution. At a later date, the same opportunities were explored with Old Mutual plc.

As Shivaji informs, 'Uday was the first to spot the opportunity in insurance as also mutual funds during the period 1996-99. We were the first to respond too. Our ability to act with agility set us apart from others. For instance, one day in December 2000 Uday called me at midnight, to say, 'If you are going to make an application to Insurance Regulatory and Development Authority (IRDA), we need a ₹500 crore net worth. What do you plan to do?' Our net worth at the time was only ₹400 crores. To be able to file the application by March, we decided to do a rights issue. Fulfilling these norms to enter the insurance sector was tight rope walking, but we managed it. That's how we got our ₹500 crore net worth. When insurance opened up in India around 2000-01, we were among the first ones to file an application with IRDA.

Such agility was also witnessed when Kotak Mahindra decided to prune its balance sheet by more than a half in anticipation of trouble in the financial sector, before the NBFC crisis. 'So many companies simply disappeared as they could not weather the storm,' Uday recalls.

Such agility continues to this day. In March 2017, KMB announced a strategy to double its existing customer base to 16 million in the next 18 months through launch of its purely digitally-enabled savings account, which the bank calls 811, following the government's push for a cashless economy after demonetization. It sought to enable people to open a savings account with the bank, without visiting the branch or producing physical documents.[72] The new product significantly reduced the cost of customer acquisition, compared to its regular accounts, by almost 80-90 per cent.

9. *Do What You Say*: At Kotak, actions speaking louder than words, is driven from the top. This culture manifests itself in small things, such as when the senior leadership team speaks of frugality, it actually demonstrates this through its own actions. Both Shanti and Dipak speak about their air travel choices. As Dipak states, his secretary would quite naturally book him on the cheapest flight available. It also manifests in simple practices like switching off the lights when they leave a room or Shanti choosing not to

---

[72]'Kotak Mahindra Bank's Uday Kotak Launches Purely Digital Saving Account '811'; Eyes Doubling User Base to 16 mn.' *The Financial Express*, 30 March 2017, www.financialexpress.com/industry/banking-finance/kotak-mahindra-banks-uday-kotak-launches-purely-digital-saving-account-811-eyes-doubling-user-base-to-16-mn/607784/. Accessed 4 July 2020.

switch on the air conditioner when she would come to work on Saturdays, as she would be alone at work.

There are other bigger instances of actions speaking louder than words, like when Uday had to borrow money to be able to raise capital to set up an insurance company under KMFL. The company needed to have a rights issue[73] to increase its net worth to ₹500 crores.
Uday recalls,

The rights issue meant that I had to put in money myself. I had to borrow about ₹40 crores against my shares and my home. The stock price was ₹200 when we announced the rights issue on an ex-rights basis, at ₹100. The rights issue was closing end of March. However, due to the dotcom bubble burst, the ₹200 price plummeted to ₹95 by the end of March 2001. The issue was likely to be under-subscribed. I remember going to meet Deepak Parekh at HDFC Ltd. and telling him, 'here are my shares and my home—I need 20 crores to fill the rights issue fully.' I increased what I had to put up, Deepak lent the money to close the gap and we made sure the rights issue closed. It helped me increase my stake of course, but I put everything on the line to get it done.

10. *An Open Culture*: In spite of Kotak's organizational structure, its people are not restricted by the invisible lines of hierarchy. While an open culture has largely worked

---

[73]A company may issue a rights offering to raise capital. A rights issue is an invitation to existing shareholders to purchase additional new shares in the company at a discount to the market price for a specified period. With a rights issue, because more shares are issued to the market, the stock price is diluted and will likely go down.

for the organization, it has also been otherwise at times. One of the ways in which it manifests is Uday's penchant to 'speak to people three levels below his direct reportees', which may unnerve people from other organizational cultures.

Uday elaborates his perspective on Kotak's open culture and what it means,

> It is about bringing in people who are different from what you are, but with a consistent value system in terms of being ethical and disciplined. The ability to think differently allows us to view and weigh different perspectives on the same situation. People could criticize me, I could criticize them, we could criticize each other. This is important in troubling times, because if you don't get the truth, you miss the issues which may potentially escalate.

Dipak further explains the idea of an open culture.

> It is not to humiliate or discredit anyone but intended to work for the benefit of the institution. No one can use the openness as a weapon. The idea is simply curiosity to open up new ideas and a passion to know things first-hand besides helping us to stay in touch and appreciate the diversity. The focus is on issues, not individuals.

On the down side, Dipak agrees that this open culture may have prevented some of the lateral recruits from getting used to working at Kotak Mahindra and their eventual departure.

We then get the sense of a distinctive organization,

which has managed to not only create wealth in less than two decades of its existence or 35 years of its existence as a group (when we take into account the NBFC days) but also create a unique style, culture and legacy that justifies it being termed an institution.

The moot question is: Will this institution survive its charismatic shaper? It is an open question but Uday believes that his driving purpose was to create a world class institution that lives through generations. As he says, 'If what you create does not outlive you, then you have failed.'

It is this question which we will turn to in our epilogue, besides looking at the entire concept of shapers and their institutions as we have understood them through our study of six distinct entities.

# Epilogue

Writing this epilogue for this sixth and last book of the Shapers' series, gives us an opportunity to reflect on the authors' journeys while researching and writing about India's prime institutions, including Kotak Mahindra Bank, among the highest league of India's valuable banks.

The first book on Tata Consultancy Services, which incidentally was co-authored by the same authors as this book, took us on a journey that allowed us to closely observe how values and processes, combined with goals and strategies, were institutionalized in successful Indian corporations of Generation Liberalization (Gen-L) vintage. For the six authors involved in this 'Shapers Project', the effort and partnership among them represented an amalgam of academics and practice.

This epilogue is written as a collective retrospective about the series.

When the Shapers project began two years ago, we challenged ourselves to adopt a rigorous research methodology. We were also keen to influence practice through theory by contributing new knowledge on Indian business practices.

We have placed within each book the research methodology that the project team adopted. There have been excellent and much-lauded book publications over the last three decades about successful companies—*In Search of Excellence, Good to Great* and *Built to Last,* among others. Each book adopted its own methodology. We were inspired by these books during our journey.

## AN ALGORITHMIC TRAP

All these books sought to study and comment on the top performing companies—a measure of their efficiency— against a peer set through meticulous analytics. It is possible to argue the view that the Anglo-Saxon mindset places efficiency on a pedestal, whereas the Indian view places effectiveness a tad higher than efficiency. Efficiency and effectiveness are not the same. Efficiency is highly focused on shareholder value, while effectiveness has a broader remit towards all stakeholders. This is not a trivial distinction.

The companies studied by foreign authors were largely American, with occasional reference to European companies. In line with good design principles, they tended to study target companies in comparison to matched paired companies. These studies attempted to define the formula or secret sauce, though, in all fairness, none of them explicitly said so. Whether or not the authors so intended it, the reader tended to accept the findings like a prescription of medicine, which could deliver targeted results if administered efficiently, a bit like an algorithm.

The fact is that management is *not* algorithmic like the physical sciences. An algorithm is formulaic, a methodical set of steps, that can be followed to solve problems and reach a decision. An algorithm will deliver the same result if it is used more than once, for example, the laws of gravity or arithmetic.

In presenting these six books, the authors recognize the algorithmic trap. Despite our sound research methodology, we feel that we have deciphered not only a combination of factors, but have also observed how the combination has been hard-wired into the organization through institutional practices. Will they work forever? Not by any means, but they will work for a decade or two, for sure.

## CONVERGENCE OF IDEAS

*In Search of Excellence* referred to the McKinsey 7S framework and posited eight attributes of the companies.[74] According to that book, companies with a passion for excellence have a bias for action, stick to the knitting, emphasize on productivity through people and so on. This book focused on a wide range of companies, both recent and long-established.

*Built to Last* sought 'timeless companies.[75] It avoided identifying the common characteristics of the companies, an analysis which may not be meaningful. As the authors argued, if a set of companies had an impressive building, this common feature could surely not be considered as a feature of Built to Last companies.

An eponymous book titled *Good to Great* was published in 2001.[76] For this book, the author assembled a 21-strong research team that discovered the technique by which chosen

---

[74]Peters, Thomas J., and Robert H. Waterman. *In Search of Excellence*. Harper & Row, 1982.
[75]Collins, James C., and Jerry I. Porras. *Built to Last: Successful Habits of Visionary Companies*. Harper Business, 1994.
[76]Collins, Jim. *Good to Great: Why Some Companies Make the Leap ... and Others Don't*. Random House, 2001.

companies achieved 'stock returns which were 6.9 times the stock market average in 15 years.' The companies, which made the leap, had some commonalities—they never lost faith and they identified the simplicity within three overlapping concentric circles: what you are passionate about, what you do best in the world and what drives your economic engine.

*Success Built to Last* introduced the concept of a 'builder'.[77] A builder, according to this book, worked at the intersection of three elements: meaning, thought and action style. Those who operated at the common intersection of these three circles were the builders, according to the authors. In our opinion, this idea is an attractive feature of the book. This study did not use the pairing principle, its focus was on the builder rather than the building, unlike our study which was more concerned with the institution rather than the shaper.

Our book series learnt from the research design and findings of these books. Indeed, we learnt from several other published papers from academic journals. Good research encourages the building of new knowledge on the foundations of existing knowledge—naturally, by accepting or rejecting certain features. We have attempted to do so and hope that our work will encourage other researchers to challenge these ideas and build further knowledge.

In our way of thinking, the following distinctive aspects have been built into the design:

i.   We researched and wrote on the experience of Indian companies, rooted and grown in the indigenous ecosystem. One can find a syncretic management

---

[77]Emery, Stewart, et al. *Success Built to Last*. Wharton Publishing, 2007.

practice in India combining Indian social values with western management ideas. Indian managers inherit an ancient entrepreneurial or trading tradition, a rich panoply of social culture, warts and all, the most diverse racial and linguistic tapestry in the world, all of which have survived through centuries of empire and colonialism. Modern Indian managers are academically trained professionals, comfortable in the English language and Anglo-Saxon management ideas. In another book, the authors have referred to this as 'Thinking in English but acting in Indian.'[78]

ii.   Indian managers, for better or worse, are less process-oriented than others in the world and tend to be far more relationship-oriented. This feature has organizational implications. In a separate book, the Indian manager was explored by two authors, associated with S. P. Jain Institute of Management and Research (SPJIMR).

iii.  Indian managers display entrepreneurship under a complex web of regulations, constraints and low-cost type of competition. This continues even after liberalization, though these are less constraining than they were in the pre-liberalization years. That is why we chose Gen-L companies. Storied house names like Tata Steel, Indian Hotels, Godrej Soaps and ITC were not considered. We also omitted multinationals, for whom the Indian subsidiary is greatly influenced by global practices.

-----

[78]Gopalakrishnan, R., and R. Banerjee. *The Made-in-India Manager*. Hachette India, 2018.

iv.   Family-managed businesses dominate the Indian business landscape. Their working is much influenced by relationships, ambiguity and intuition. This has positives and negatives. We sought and found fine institutions, which had sprung from family roots, but which delicately disengaged from family to create highly professional organizations.

v.    We sought Indian companies whose record of ethical business is top-class and who are acknowledged for practicing globally competitive corporate governance.

The academic literature search developed into the Mindset, Behaviour, Action (MBA) grid; the eight MBAs have been described in our books. Through our interviews, we found that institution shapers all resorted to the first three MBAs. Of the remaining five, each shaper resorted to different choices and approaches.

This observation led to our 3 + 5 hypothesis as being the MBAs toolkit: Three essentials plus five variables. In a sense, this resonated with the emergence principle insofar as there was no algorithmic approach, but a delicate case by case choice from the toolkit. Naturally this stacks up with commonsense and experience as well.

Our readers will not find a formula anywhere in the book. Rather, readers will find a hymn sheet (the MBA grid) with multiple ways of expressing the music, depending on the orchestra players and their distinctive concert. We regard this as the strength of these six books, all of which the reader would do well to read.

This epilogue is best closed on that pitch!

# Research Methodology: Shaper's MBA Grid

A section on research approach and methodology seems out of place in a practice-oriented book, which aims to guide the modern-day manager and leader to be the Shaper of an organization that can outlive most of its peers and be hailed as an institution through its actions. While the book aims to be practitioner relevant—given the ambitious goal of studying six different organizations recognized as institutions in India and discerning patterns—the research project was guided by a theoretical construct, which was the result of serious deliberation and iteration. We termed this construct the **'Shaper's MBA Grid'**, which is an important contribution, as it has the potential to act as a beacon for other researchers interested or working in the field of leadership and organizational behaviour in the Indian context.

As such, we decided to 'relegate' the research approach and methodology to an appendix section, rather than use a book chapter for the same. The advantage of an appendix is that it can be skipped by those disinterested in the research approach itself without much loss of continuity in narrative. At the same time, it seemed apt to present serious researchers—who seek to further the research agenda on the theory and practice of institution-building—with a thorough understanding of the mindset and action patterns of institution builders.

Again, unlike the conventional research methodology section in an academic paper, we shall seek to keep this section light, highlighting the 'What', 'Why' and 'How' of our research in language that will appeal to the lay reader as much as to the seasoned academic.

## THE 'WHAT'

The Shapers Research project owes its genesis to a serendipitous discussion amongst a few SPJIMR faculty members in 2018 on the distinction between organizations and institutions and the distinction between their leaders. Discussion veered around Indian companies that feature in the Fortune Global 2000 list. There were about 50, including those like Reliance Industries (in the top 200 list) and TCS (in the top 500 list). There was consensus—tentative at this stage—that not all these organizations were 'institutions'. Also, while these organizations are aspirational to several MBA students who seek to find jobs with them, they offer little hope to the sceptic who is convinced about the mortality of corporations.

An influential piece of research in 2012 by Professor Richard Foster from Yale University, for instance, posited that the average lifespan of a company listed in the S&P 500 index of leading US companies has decreased by more than 50 years in the last century—from 67 years in the 1920s to just 15 years today.[79] Another study found the timespan of business survival to be merely 10 years.[80]

Given that most Indian businesses have emerged post the opening up of the Indian economy in 1991 and yet face multiple business challenges in the current uncertain and volatile business environment, the question that emerged was: 'Which of these organizations will survive long enough? Which Indian businesses are institutions?'

At this stage, we defined the term 'Institution' itself as an organization that had, at its core, certain universally accepted values and norms for which it was revered; an organization that had withstood the test of time—having been established within a decade or two since Independence—and seemed to possess an innate resilience to be able to withstand multiple business challenges, having already survived several such challenges in the last several decades.

As we began to identify some of the organizations that qualified as institutions, as well as the factors that distinguished them from others, a Eureka moment came in the realisation that the phenomenon of institution-building is deeply linked to the leadership experience that each one goes through. In particular, we realized that the hypotheses for the research project, were it a conventional one, could very well read as follows:

**H1:** The number of years an organization survives is linked

---

[79]Kim, Kevin. 'Can a Company Live Forever? *'BBC News,* 19 January 2012, www.bbc.com/news/business-16611040. Accessed 4 July 2020.
[80]'This is How Long Your Business Will Last, According to Science.' *Fortune,* 2 Apr. 2015, fortune.com/2015/04/02/this-is-how-long-your-business-will-last-according-to-science/. Accessed 4 July 2020.

positively to leadership performance.

**H2:** The ability of an organization to withstand business volatility and severe business challenges is linked positively to leadership performance.

**H3:** The reputation that an organization carries is linked positively to leadership performance.
Needless to say, our preliminary research into institutions was guided by a literature review of scholarly work on institution-building, ranging from Powell, Arie de Geus, Di Maggio, Meyers and Rowan to Indian scholars like Udai Pareek.

This then led to the question: What sort of leadership performance will qualify for such transformation of ordinary organizations into venerated institutions? The obvious answer was 'Transformational' leadership of a sort that transcends the current notion of leadership, as enunciated by Goleman, Moss Kanter and others—a leadership that not only transforms, but rather 'shapes' the organization into an institution. Such leaders may be called 'Shapers.' We also realized that just as there are only a few organizations that may make it to a list of 'institutions,' there are only a few business leaders who may qualify as 'Shapers' of institutions.

This led us to an additional hypothesis:

**H4:** Leadership mindsets, behaviours and actions undertaken by 'Shapers' are unique and distinct from those of Leaders.

We thought we were on to something interesting with this discovery. The next obvious question was: Could we—a group of interested researchers—work on a set of Indian organizations that *we* could identify as institutions, using a commonly accepted set of parameters? The set of such institutions need not be exhaustive. However, they need to conform to the parameters laid out, and should not be deemed questionable by the set of researchers working on the project, which now had a name—the SPJIMR SHAPERS PROJECT. Can such institution-building be studied in the context of the leaders, who, as Shapers, shaped and created them in a manner such that they have become enduring? Could we study and glean a set of uniform mindsets, behaviours and actions that would set these leaders apart from other leaders who are non-Shapers? And how do these Shapers shape their organizations into institutions?

This then leads to the second aspect of our research: Why did we want to do this?

## THE 'WHY'

Well, we could advance a large number of great-sounding explanations for why we undertook this research project—explanations such as: 'We wanted to understand the mindsets and actions of Shapers so that it can help create Shapers for the future.' Or, 'We want to make a difference to Indian management discipline and practice.'

These reasons are valid and good reasons to conduct any such research. However, as every well-intentioned researcher in the field of social science will testify: We undertake research when the theme excites us. It helps us uncover phenomenon of which we have little understanding but wish to unravel for ourselves. In the process, we do help set the research agenda for others as well.

In this case, it made sense, as we could discern hints of a pattern emerging even as we began to do our preliminary research based on secondary data. We realized that rather than talking about leadership types in an anecdotal fashion, we could possibly decipher a method to such transformational leadership—not consciously agreed upon by those who practice it, but present all the same, waiting to be discovered and possibly even replicated.

In particular, what excited us were questions like this:

- How does one distinguish an institution from an organization, even if the key metrics used to map organizational performance are similar—that is, involve deeper qualitative questions than merely looking at quantitative metrics? Thus, for instance, why should Reliance not feature in our list, even though it is one of the top Indian companies on the Fortune Global 2000 list?
- What transforms an organization into an institution? (The emphasis was on the process and not the outcomes.)
- What mindsets, behaviours and actions set a Shaper apart from a leader? This would entail a deep qualitative analysis, which could form the basis for a new theoretical construct, called the 'Shaper' construct.
- How and when does a leader qualify as a Shaper?

These questions also became the 'Why' or the 'purpose' of our research. In the process, if we are able to expedite the transformation of some business organizations into institutions through their leaders adopting the right 'Shaper' mindset, that will be a happy, albeit unintentional, consequence of this book and project.

This leads us to our final question: How did we manage to undertake and bring to fruition this project?

## THE 'HOW'

The process of shortlisting the tentative candidate organizations for the research project was undertaken by a small group, comprising the authors—including the lead author, R. Gopalakrishnan—and Ranjan Banerjee, the Dean of SPJIMR. A set of six institutions were initially shortlisted, with the understanding that a second round of other institutions could be worked on at a later stage. The institutions shortlisted in the first round included, in alphabetical order: Biocon, HDFC, Kotak, L&T, Marico and TCS.

Each of the co-authors, well-respected academics in their own right, began with carrying out background research on their subject of study—both the Shaper and the institution. In the case of the book on TCS, we researched two Shapers for the same institution.

We deliberated, discussed, and arrived at the idea of a 'framework' that could be used to explore the main hypotheses. This was named the SPJIMR MBA Grid. The contents of the grid itself were arrived at through an iterative process of refinement as the research progressed.

In the initial stage, the grid was visualized as a 9×9 matrix with Managers, Leaders and Shapers as distinct agents along task and process dimensions. The task dimensions considered were: Managing the Core; Preparing the Future; and Creating the Future. Along the process dimension, managers were hypothesized as focusing on Policies and Processes; Leaders as focusing on Performance, while Shapers would focus on

People. Juxtaposing the task and process dimensions, we arrived at a set of nine unique actions, which would set apart Shapers from Leaders and Managers.

In Stage 2, we refined this further to arrive at an 8×3 matrix. The vertical dimension (the columns) looked at Mindset, Behaviour and Actions, while the horizontal dimension (the rows) looked at the MBA dimensions broadly based on the 4Ps: Purpose, People, Policies and Processes. A Shaper was identified in terms of his or her mindset along eight dimensions: People Relations, Short-term and Long-term Focus, Critical Thinking, Orbit Shifting, Breaking Barriers, Levers of Change, Cyclical Learning and Stakeholder Orientation. We have provided these characteristics in the detailed MBA grid below.

The next step was to seek in-depth interviews with the 'Shapers' of these institutions, as also with multiple stakeholders, who could shed light on various dimensions of the Shaper in question and their institution. While we decided and planned for the interviews, the idea was clear: These books were not meant to be hagiographies. While there were protagonists within the case study approach who were the Shapers, the 'heroes' were clearly the institutions, which had withstood the test of time and made distinct contributions to nation-building. Again, it was a conscious decision not to attempt to discuss the warts et al. of the Shapers, the reason being that we are interested in understanding the positive mindset that contributes to the building of a Shaper—an individual who, despite largely having an unblemished track record, is nevertheless as human as any of us in terms of frailties and vulnerabilities. Nowhere, then, should the book be construed as an attempt to idolize a human being with a larger-than-life image.

Each researcher conducted at least three such interviews with different people associated with the Shaper and/or the institution in question. Some of us met our protagonists more than once as well. The questions used to test the hypotheses included some generic questions, and others that were specific to the particular institution or Shaper. They included questions which revolved around institution-building, such as:

- How did you set the organizational vision, values and performance expectations?
- How do you attract, retain and enhance talent within your organization?
- What is the leadership's purpose? How do you communicate with your workforce?
- How do you arrive at and institutionalize the core values of the organization?
- What is the role of 'out-of-box' thinking and an entrepreneurial mindset for any organization? How do you ensure that such a mindset gets internalized into the DNA of the institution?
- How do you and your senior leadership team guide and sustain the organization?
- How do you develop future leaders, measure organizational performance and create an environment that encourages ethical behaviour and high performance?
- What are the institution's core competencies, work systems and designs that help to create value for your customers?
- How do you identify the organization's blind spots

in achieving long-term organizational success and sustainability?

- What specific processes in institution-building have you undertaken?
- How have you addressed succession planning in your organization?

There were other questions pertaining to each Shaper, which sought to explore key facets of their life that helped 'shape' the Shaper, starting from childhood, as well as their role models. Another interesting question posed to the Shapers was: What if they were given another three to five more years at the helm? What would be the key 'unfinished' agenda that they would want to address?

All these questions helped glean the Shaper mindset, behaviour and actions relating to specific aspects of institution building. We probed three specific areas: building the institution (sometimes from scratch), seeing it through troubled times and changing the course. The idea was threefold: understanding the context, understanding the leader and understanding the institution.

The chapters have also been aligned accordingly: The initial chapters set the context in which the organization developed, while the next set of chapters look at the life and key influences on the Shaper, as also specific aspects of the Shaper's mindset, behaviour and actions. The last set of chapters covers the institution—what makes it qualify as one, the salient features of an institution, and understanding the future of the institution.

| SPJIMR SHAPER MINDSET-BEHAVIOR-ACTION GRID | | |
|---|---|---|
| Mindset | Behaviour | Action |
| People relations: Respectful to others | Sensitive and empathetic to others | Engages with people and nurtures them |
| Short vs long term: Both are equally important | Encourages to deal with the immediate, while silently considering the long term | Acts on the immediate decisively to get results, creating the impression of small wins, so as to look forward to and work towards a big 'victory' in the future |
| Critical thinking: Considers options and their pros/cons in mental evaluation | Encourages discussion and debate with open-mindedness | Acts with precision and demands accountability |
| Orbit Changing: Constant evaluation of which orbit change will benefit the organization | Tosses around and debates the risks and rewards of orbit change, almost appearing indecisive | Demonstrates single-minded commitment once a decision is made |
| Break Barriers: I have the freedom to act if I am willing to steer through obstacles | Identifies the obstacles and seeks the best way to deal with them— break them, go around them, navigate them | Once the path is clear, pursues with an Arjuna-like determination |
| Levers of change: Action is within my reach: must change complacency to the aspirational mindset | Debates and seeks ways to dislodge the organization from negative hooks while attaching positive hooks | Presses for action and change in a disciplined manner |
| Cyclical learning: Action-Observation-Benchmark-Review-Act again | Insists on a systems approach of cyclical learning | Ensures organization-wide deployment of an accepted system |
| Stakeholder Orientation: What is good for the stakeholder is good for the institution and hence, for us | Constantly understanding customer and community perspective | Always acts by keeping in mind multiple stakeholder interests |

# Acknowledgements

Family, friends, colleagues and others have certainly played a role in the shaping of this project and in the writing of this book as well as the earlier ones in the series. In fact, but for their unstinted support, this book would never have been.

We thank the publishers—Rupa, who reposed confidence in a book series of this sort. The Rupa team that patiently worked with the six shapers of this book, deserves special mention.

We thank the Shaper, Uday Kotak, who spared his time to speak with us and narrate personal anecdotes and life experiences, which have found their way into this book. Others who generously gave their time and helped to provide information for this book include Uday's father, Suresh Kotak, his friend, Amit Desai, members of his senior management team (past and current) including Dipak Gupta, Shivaji Dam, Jayaram, Jaimin Bhatt, Shanti Ekambaram, G. Muralidhar, Narayan S.A. and Gaurang Shah, who gave us deeper insights into the mindset, behaviour and actions of the shaper, as also the context in which Kotak Mahindra was shaped.

To Dean, Ranjan Banerjee, we owe the environment of discussion and debate, which helped 'shape' this series, and to Dr Manesh Shrikant, our Late Dean, to whom we owe the institution namely SPJIMR.

Tulsi thanks Anant Narayan who was originally supposed

to have written this book, and who undertook some of the spade work through the initial set of interviews. In fact, she views this book as a serendipitous journey- one she has enjoyed, and which has ensured that the first and the last book of the six-book series both carry her name as co-author. She also wishes to thank the library staff at SPJIMR—Mallappa Kumbar and Sanjay Narvekar, who have always helped scour all literature required for reference purposes.

And finally, we owe a debt of gratitude to our families. Geeta—Gopalakrishnan's wife, and Jay and Radhika—Tulsi's husband and daughter respectively—who have provided the emotional support at all times and have kept up the faith. Tulsi wishes to dedicate this book to the three women in her life, who have at various points of time in her life been her 'Shapers'—her mother, Kalpakam, her mother-in-law, Jayam and her Chitti (aunt), Kamakshi.

# Index

www.ingramcontent.com/pod-product-compliance
Lightning Source LLC
Chambersburg PA
CBHW031359180326
41458CB00043B/6547/J